WASHINGTON–BALTIMORE
SPORTS
QUIZ

WASHINGTON–BALTIMORE SPORTS QUIZ

Brenda Alesii
&
Daniel Locche

A Citadel Press Book
Published by Carol Publishing Group

A Citadel Press Book
Published by Carol Publishing Group

Citadel Press is a registered trademark of Carol
Communications, Inc.

Editorial Offices: 600 Madison Avenue, New York, N.Y. 10022
Sales & Distribution Offices: 120 Enterprise Avenue, Secaucus,
   N.J. 07094
In Canada: Canadian Manda Group, P.O. Box 920, Station U,
   Toronto, Ontario M8Z 5P9

Queries regarding rights and permissions should be addressed to
Carol Publishing Group, 600 Madison Avenue, New York, N.Y. 10022

Carol Publishing Group books are available at special discounts
for bulk purchases, for sales promotions, fund-raising, or
educational purposes. Special editions can be created to specifications.
For details, contact Special Sales Department, Carol Publishing
Group, 120 Enterprise Avenue, Secaucus, N.J. 07094

Manufactured in the United States of America
10   9   8   7   6   5   4   3   2   1

Library of Congress Cataloging-in-Publication Data

Alesii, Brenda.
    Washington–Baltimore sports quiz: Senators, Orioles, Redskins.
  Colts, Bullets, Capitals / by Brenda Alesii and Daniel Locche.
        p.   cm.
     "A Citadel Press book."
     ISBN 0–8065–1424–8
     1. Sports–Washington (D.C.)—Miscellanea.   2. Sports—Maryland–
  Baltimore—Miscellanea.   I. Locche, Daniel.   II. Title.
  GV854.5.W37A44   1993
  796'.09753—dc20   92–38083
                                                                CIP

Contents

Acknowledgments

Washington–Baltimore Sports Quiz is the fifth in our line of sports trivia books. Preceding this edition are *New York Sports Quiz, Boston Sports Quiz, Chicago Sports Quiz,* and *Los Angeles Sports Quiz.* We are well on our way to producing a series of books detailing the sports facts and histories in selected cities throughout the United States and Canada.

Our goal for each book is simple. We attempt to provide an entertaining and informative compilation of particular cities' "big four" major league teams under one cover. Included in every edition are offbeat, fascinating, and intriguing aspects of pro sports, as well as a statistical chronicle of the franchises.

We derive great pleasure from writing the books because of our almost obsessive love of sports, our desire to travel, and the mutual enjoyment of working together. (Yes, we are a husband-and-wife team that actually relishes working together!) We've weathered some long nights and snowy roads in our effort to put together a product that we can be proud of, one that we hope will settle some arguments, start a few, and provide endless hours of enjoyment.

The friendships that developed from the production of our books are the greatest reward of all. Many thanks to the following for their assistance, guidance, and counsel:

Bob Salomon and Al Marill of Carol Publishing Group
Tom Hietz and the staff at the Baseball Hall of Fame
Wayne Patterson and the staff at the Basketball Hall of Fame
Joe Horrigan, Pete Fierle, Sandy Self, and the staff at the
Football Hall of Fame
Phil Pritchart and the staff at the Hockey Hall of Fame
The Orioles, Senators, Bullets, Capitals, Redskins, and Colts
Our families and friends who offer unwavering support and
tolerate us as our deadline approaches.

Photos included in this book were obtained from the following
sources:
Basketball: Hall of Fame, Springfield, Massachusetts
Baseball: National Baseball Library, Cooperstown, New York
Football: Hall of Fame, Canton, Ohio, and NFL Properties
Hockey: Hall of Fame, Toronto, Ontario, Canada

Dedication

This book is dedicated to the memory of Anthony B. Locche, a man who deeply loved sports, and a man who was loved deeply by his family and the countless friends who had the privilege to make his acquaintance.

How to Use
Washington–Baltimore
Sports Quiz

Washington–Baltimore Sports Quiz is divided into six chapters: the Redskins, Colts, Orioles, Senators, Capitals, and Bullets. Each section contains questions, answers, and "fast facts" pertaining to the particular team.

For your convenience, the question page always precedes the answer page; questions are grouped separately from their respective answers. (A "Q" represents a question, while an "A" indicates an answer.) Each chapter reflects the chronology of the team. It is divided into separate categories in the following manner: "Suits" denotes coaches, managers, and front-office personnel; "Uniforms" involves the players; "Setting the Standard" is about records; "FYI" is general information; "Glory Days" covers the playoffs and any postseason activity; and "Trades, Waives, and Acquisitions" are just that.

The questions are current as of February 1993.

As is generally recognized, the Baltimore–Washington area is home to some of the most knowledgeable sports fans in the country. In compiling the hundreds of questions and answers, we may have overlooked some facts and figures. We ask your indulgence.

If you have a particular bit of information to add or would like to discuss the contents of *Washington—Baltimore Sports Quiz*, we encourage you to contact us.

Baltimore Orioles

BALTIMORE ORIOLES

FAN APPRECIATION NIGHT 9/27/66.

TADDER BALTIMORE

1966 BALTIMORE ORIOLES

Back Row: Eddie Fisher, Moe Drabowsky, John Miller, Jim Palmer, Dick Hall, Gene Brabender, Curt Blefary, Wally Bunker, Steve Barber, Woody Held, Frank Robinson. Middle Row: Ralph Salvon — Trainer, Eddie Weidner — Trainer, Dave Johnson, Eddie Watt, Charlie Lau, Frank Bertaina, Sam Bowens, Larry Haney, Vic Roznovsky, Paul Blair, Andy Etchebarren, Bob Johnson. Clay Reid — Equipment Manager. Front Row: Stu Miller, Luis Aparicio, Dave McNally, Harry Brecheen, Billy Hunter, Hank Bauer, Gene Woodling, Sherm Lollar, Russ Snyder, Brooks Robinson. Boog Powell.   Bobby Sherr — Batboy.

- - 10 -

THE SUITS

Q1   What Oriole manager once held the record (since broken) of managing the most seasons (21) without winning a pennant?

Q2   Who has the best win-loss percentage of any Oriole manager?

Q3   Who was Baltimore's first general manager?

Q4   What well-known baseball man sold the St. Louis Browns to a group of Baltimore businessmen in 1954?

Q5   What two teams did Jimmy Dykes manage prior to coming to Baltimore in 1954?

Q6   In Jimmy Dykes's 21 years as manager, what was the highest standing that any of his clubs finished?

Q7   Paul Richards was a catcher with what world championship club?

Q8   Why did Paul Richards resign as manager of the Orioles on August 30, 1961?

Q9   What piece of Baseball equipment did Paul Richards design while managing the Orioles?

Q10   What Oriole battery influenced Paul Richards to invent new baseball equipment?

Q11   Fifteen years after leaving the O's, Paul Richards took one more turn as a major league manager. What club took the 59-year-old in 1976?

BALTIMORE ORIOLES

A1   Jimmy Dykes

A2   Luman Harris (August 30, 1961 through September 30, 1961: 17–10, .630)

A3   Arthur Ehlers

A4   Bill Veeck

A5   Chicago White Sox (1934–46)
Philadelphia Athletics (1951–53)

A6   Third (Three times; in contrast, his clubs finished last seven times.)

A7   Detroit Tigers (1945)

A8   He took the position of general manager for the new Houston Colt 45s franchise.

A9   The "pillow" (oversized) catching mitt (It was outlawed by the Playing Rules Committee because it was too big.)

A10   Pitcher Hoyt Wilhelm
Catcher Gus Triandos
(Wilhelm's butterfly pitch was difficult to catch, so Richards came up with a mitt with a 45-inch circumference.)

A11   Chicago White Sox (He compiled a 64–97 record in his one and only season.)

Q12 Paul Richards held the dual titles of manager and general manager with Baltimore from 1955 to 1958. In 1958, he retained his title as field manager, but the position was taken away. Who took over the administrative post?

Q13 Who succeeded Paul Richards on August 30, 1961, and finished out the 1961 Oriole season?

Q14 At what university did Billy Hitchcock distinguish himself as a baseball and football star?

Q15 Billy Hitchcock had an undistinguished nine-year career as a major leaguer. With what four clubs did the infielder play?

Q16 What two teams did Billy Hitchcock manage besides the Orioles?

Q17 After being relieved of his managerial duties in 1963, Billy Hitchcock was given another position within the Oriole organization. What was it?

Q18 Hank Bauer's playing career is best known for his years with the Yankees—12 seasons, nine pennants, seven World Series. With what club did the outfielder end his playing career?

Q19 What position with the Orioles did Hank Bauer hold prior to being named manager in 1964?

Q20 Prior to hiring Hank Bauer as the Oriole manager in 1964, owner Dan Topping expressed interest in two other men to lead the club. Who were choices one and two?

Q21 How many times did Hank Bauer win Manager of the Year honors while at the Oriole helm?

Q22 In a unique honor, Hank Bauer adorned the cover of what national publication on September 11, 1964?

Q23 Second baseman Earl Weaver was a member of the Cardinal and Pirate organizations for nine years. In how many major league games did he play?

Q24 How old was Earl Weaver when he was named manager of the O's in 1968?

Q25 How long was Earl Weaver's first managerial contract with the Orioles?

Q26 What significance does Larry Napp hold in Earl Weaver's big league managerial career?

BALTIMORE ORIOLES

A12   Lee MacPhail

A13   Luman Harris

A14   Auburn

A15   Detroit Tigers (1942, 1946, 1953)
St. Louis Browns (1947)
Boston Red Sox (1948–49)
Philadelphia Athletics (1950–52)

A16   Detroit Tigers (1960)
Atlanta Braves (1966–67)

A17   Field coordinator (The primary responsibilities of his new job were scouting major league teams, coaching at spring training, and general troubleshooting.)

A18   Kansas City Athletics (1960–1961)

A19   Third base coach

A20   1 - Yogi Berra (The Yankees would not give Topping permission to talk with Berra, since they were about to name him as their manager.)
2 - Eddie Stanky (He was rejected because he wanted a long-term contract.)

A21   Twice (1964 and 1966)

A22   *Time*

A23   None

A24   38 years old (At the time, he was the youngest manager in the American League.)

A25   Two and a half months (He was appointed manager on July 11, 1968, and his contract ran to the end of that season.)

A26   Napp was the first umpire to eject Weaver from a baseball game. (September 2, 1968)

Q27 Earl Weaver was ejected for the 94th and last time in his career on June 11, 1986, in a game against Milwaukee. Who was the last ump to thumb Weaver?

Q28 For the 17 years that Earl Weaver managed the Birds, he espoused a certain philosophy. For what old saw was Weaver known?

Q29 Earl Weaver called it quits in 1982, but returned to managing halfway through the 1985 season. In 1986 Weaver experienced something for the first time. What was it?

Q30 After a two-and-a-half-year hiatus, Earl Weaver returned on June 14, 1985, to replace Joe Altobelli as Oriole manager. Who did Baltimore defeat to celebrate his return?

Q31 What song was played over the Memorial Stadium public-address system when Earl Weaver returned to manage the Orioles on June 14, 1985?

Q32 What was the last team Earl Weaver managed against?

Q33 Earl Weaver had five 100-victory seasons with the Orioles. Who is the only manager in major league history to have more?

Q34 What club selected Earl Weaver's son Mike in the 1969 free agent draft?

Q35 Name the Baltimore general manager who fired Hank Bauer at the 1968 All-Star break.

Q36 With what club did Joe Altobelli earn Manager of the Year honors?

Q37 Following the Orioles' 1984 season, GM Hank Peters began to search for a replacement for Joe Altobelli because of Baltimore's 85–77 record and fifth-place finish. Who did Peters initially approach?

Q38 True or false—in the two and a half years that Joe Altobelli managed the club, the Orioles never fell below .500.

Q39 Cal Ripken, Sr.'s debut as Oriole manager actually took place on June 13, 1986, when he was interim manager for one game between Joe Altobelli and Earl Weaver. What club did Baltimore defeat that evening?

Q40 April 12, 1988, was a bad day for Cal Ripken, Sr. Besides being fired as the Orioles' manager, what else happened to him?

BALTIMORE ORIOLES

A27   Rocky Roe

A28   "If you play for one run, that's all you get."

A29   Weaver sustained his first-ever losing season (73–89; .451).

A30   Milwaukee Brewers (9–3)

A31   "Welcome Back" (the theme song from the television show "Welcome Back, Kotter," sung by John Sebastian.)

A32   Detroit Tigers (October 5, 1986: Detroit won 6–3, in Baltimore.)

A33   Joe McCarthy, with six

A34   Seattle Pilots (The young Weaver never signed with the club.)

A35   Harry Dalton

A36   San Francisco Giants (1979)

A37   John McNamara (McNamara was interested in the Red Sox managerial post and turned Peters down, so the GM decided to go with Altobelli one more year.)

A38   False. The Orioles were sub-.500 for 29 games (including opening day) out of the 379 games that he managed. His career record with the club is 212–167—a .559 win-loss percentage.

A39   Milwaukee Brewers (8–3, at Memorial Stadium)

A40   He pleaded guilty to a drunken-driving charge that morning, was fined $750, and was placed on three years' probation in Baltimore County District Court.

Q41 GM and vice president Roland Hemond joined the Oriole organization on November 10, 1987, and immediately began to rebuild the club. Within one month, he made his first trade for Baltimore. Who did Hemond acquire in his initial deal?

Q42 Frank Robinson's playing career spanned 21 years and five teams. Name the clubs he played for.

Q43 While playing with the Reds in 1959, Frank Robinson slid hard into third base in a game against Milwaukee. The result was one of the largest brawls in baseball history—both benches cleared and police had to be called onto the field. What future Hall of Famer played third base for the Braves that day?

Q44 Frank Robinson tied a major league record when he belted 38 homers as a rookie in 1956. Whose mark did he equal?

Q45 Name the Cincinnati general manager who dealt Frank Robinson to the Orioles in 1965.

Q46 In that swap, one of the most unpopular moves in Cincinnati baseball history, the Reds traded Frank Robinson and Dick Simpson to the Orioles. What pair of pitchers went to the Buckeye State in the 1965 deal?

Q47 In his first season with the O's, Frank Robinson won the Triple Crown. Who was the last player before Robinson to have won it?

Q48 Only one player has captured the Triple Crown since Frank Robinson won it in 1966. Name him.

Q49 In Frank Robinson's first season with the Orioles, his career and life almost came to an end when he nearly drowned after a swimming pool accident. Name the teammate who saved the Hall of Famer's life.

Q50 Frank Robinson suffered from double vision for a year and a half following a collision in a June 1967 game. With whom did the Oriole's star collide?

Q51 What was distinctive about Frank Robinson winning the American League MVP award in 1966?

Q52 Frank Robinson ranks third in major league history for being hit by pitches in a career (198). Who is ahead of him?

Q53 On June 26, 1970, Frank Robinson became the seventh player in major league history to belt two grand slams in one game. Against what club did Robinson hit them?

BALTIMORE ORIOLES

A41   Pitcher Doug Sisk (He sent Greg Talamantez and Blaine Beatty to the Mets for the right-handed pitcher.)

A42   Cincinnati Reds (1956–65)
Baltimore Orioles (1966–71)
L.A. Dodgers (1972)
California Angels (1973–74)
Cleveland Indians (1974–76)

A43   Eddie Mathews

A44   Wally Berger's (1930: Boston Braves)

A45   Bill DeWitt (DeWitt eventually lost his job due to the one-sided deal.)

A46   Milt Pappas
Jack Baldschun

A47   Mickey Mantle (1956)

A48   Carl Yastrzemski (1967)

A49   Charlie Lau

A50   White Sox' Al Weis

A51   Robinson was the first man to win the award in both the AL and NL. (He won the NL honor in 1961 with the Reds.)

A52   Don Baylor (267)
Ron Hunt (243)

A53   Washington Senators (Robinson hit the dingers in consecutive innings off pitchers Joe Coleman and Joe Grzenda.)

Q54   Frank Robinson was the first black manager in the history of major league baseball. With what team did he break into the managerial ranks?

Q55   Since 1959, there have been only five ML playing managers. Frank Robinson was a player/manager with the Indians form 1975 through 1977. Name the other four men who have split their responsibilities since that time.

Q56   Frank Robinson played in his last big league game on September 18, 1976, as a pinch hitter. In his last at-bat, he hit a single and picked up an RBI. What pitcher was on the mound for Robinson's last turn at the plate?

Q57   When Frank Robinson was appointed manager of the O's in 1988, it was the fourth time that a black was selected for that post on a major league club (including Robinson's first tenure). Besides Robinson, what others had been chosen to that position?

Q58   The first time in major league history that two black managers faced each other in a game occurred on June 27, 1989. Frank Robinson was at the helm of the Orioles that day. Who was the opposing manager?

Q59   Johnny Oates was drafted and signed by the Orioles in 1967. He was selected the previous year by another major league team, but he did not sign with them. What club originally drafted the catcher?

Q60   What four clubs did Johnny Oates play with besides the Orioles?

Q61   In October 1975, Johnny Oates, representing the National League, lost a championship title to Milwaukee's Kurt Bevacqua, the AL delegate. What was the contest?

THE UNIFORMS

Q1   Who is the oldest player to don an Oriole uniform?

Q2   Before coming to the Orioles, this player was named Rookie of the Year and MVP in the same season—the only player to ever earn both honors in the same season. Name him.

Q3   Name the onetime Oriole who can claim that he is the only player to be a teammate of both Hank Aaron and Japanese home-run king Sadaharu Oh.

BALTIMORE ORIOLES

A54   Cleveland Indians (1975: He was a player-manager.)

A55   Pete Rose (Cincinnati: 1984–86)
Joe Torre (N.Y. Mets: 1977)
Don Kessinger (Chicago White Sox: 1979)
Solly Hemus (St. Louis: 1959)

A56   Baltimore's Rudy May (Robinson was hitting for Indian Frank Duffy.)

A57   Larry Doby (White Sox: 1978)
Maury Wills (Mariners: 1980–81)

A58   Cito Gaston (Toronto Blue Jays)

A59   Chicago White Sox

A60   Atlanta Braves (1973–75)
Philadelphia Phillies (1975–76)
L.A. Dodgers (1977–79)
New York Yankees (1980–81)

A61   The first World Series of Bubble Gum Blowing

————————————   ·   ————————————

A1   Rick Dempsey (The catcher was 42 when he re-signed with the club in 1992.)

A2   Fred Lynn (1975: while playing with the Boston Red Sox)

A3   Davey Johnson

Q4   In 12 major league seasons, including four-plus years with the Orioles, this second-string catcher played for seven teams. His most notable achievement is appearing in the Mets' "How to Score" section of the Shea Stadium programs for over 20 years. Who is he?

Q5   Before coming to the Orioles, this player became the first World Series MVP to join a new team the next season. Who is he?

Q6   Identify the Baltimore pitcher who once called the press box during a game to complain about an official scorer's decision charging him with four earned runs.

Q7   What three Orioles have made the Hall of Fame in their first year of eligibility?

Q8   Prior to arriving to Baltimore, this player belted a grand slam in an All-Star Game, the first to accomplish this feat. Who is he?

Q9   Who was the last player to perform in the majors from the Orioles' forerunner, the St. Louis Browns?

Q10   Who was the last member of the St. Louis Browns to play for the Orioles?

Q11   What Oriole played in the most games in the club's first season?

Q12   Who led the Orioles in homers in the club's inaugural season?

Q13   In 1954, the first black player appeared in an Oriole box score. Who was he?

Q14   Why is second baseman Bobby Young a noteworthy name in Oriole history?

Q15   Who was named the team's Most Valuable Oriole in Baltimore's first season (1954)?

Q16   This outfielder had an undistinguished five-year career. In 1949, he led the league in strikeouts and in 1950 led the AL in errors. He played only 11 games with the '54 Orioles in his final ML season. His claim to fame was that he could throw from the outfield to home while on his knees. Name him.

Q17   Name the pitcher who had a 3–21 record during the Orioles' inaugural season, but went on to earn a place in baseball history only two years later.

Q18   Why is Duane Pillette's name in the Orioles' record books?

BALTIMORE ORIOLES

A4   Joe Ginsberg (Ginsberg was used in the programs since he was the opening day catcher for the Mets in their inaugural home game.)

A5   Ray Knight (He won the honor in the 1986 Series while playing with the Mets. He came to Baltimore in 1987.)

A6   Milt Pappas

A7   Jim Palmer
Brooks Robinson
Frank Robinson

A8   Fred Lynn (1983 All-Star Game)

A9   Don Larsen (He broke into the majors with the Browns in 1953 and lasted through the 1967 season.)

A10   Don Larsen (After playing for the Browns in 1953, he played with Baltimore in 1954, five different clubs between 1955 and 1965, and returned to the Orioles in 1965 to finish the season..)

A11   Second baseman Bobby Young (130 games)

A12   Vern Stephens, with eight

A13   Pitcher Jehosie "Jay" Heard

A14   The Maryland native was the first player signed by the Orioles after the franchise relocated from St. Louis to Baltimore in 1954.

A15   Outfielder Chuck Diering

A16   Dick Kokos

A17   Don Larsen (Larsen pitched the only World Series no-hitter in history, for the New York Yankees against the Dodgers in 1956.)

A18   Pillette chalked up the team's first-ever win, on April 14, 1954. (He went the distance in a 3–2 victory over the Tigers in Detroit.)

Q19 Brooks Robinson never played high school baseball. In what unusual setting was he discovered?

Q20 Whom did Brooks Robinson succeed at the Orioles' starting third baseman?

Q21 Brooks Robinson missed 18 games during the 1965 season when an errant pitch broke his thumb. Who was responsible for the throw?

Q22 After a brilliant performance in the 1970 World Series against the Reds, Brooks Robinson was named MVP. As a result of his play, the Reds christened him with a new nickname. What was it?

Q23 The worst defensive game ever played by Brooks Robinson occurred on July 28, 1971, when the Golden Glover committed three errors in one inning (the sixth). Against what team were the boots committed?

Q24 From 1960 through 1975, Brooks Robinson won 16 consecutive Gold Gloves as the American League's top defensive third baseman. Who beat him out for the honor in 1976?

Q25 In Brooks Robinson's illustrious 23-year career with Baltimore, he won 16 Gold Gloves and was at the hot corner in 17 All-Star Games. In how many winning All-Star Games was Brooksie involved?

Q26 When Brooks Robinson retired in 1977, he had played in 2,896 games— second most in AL history. Who played in the most American League games?

Q27 Signed by the Orioles in 1955, this former Boston College quarterback was a backup catcher for two seasons before he died in a light-plane crash in September 1956. Who was this major leaguer?

Q28 The Orioles' regular second baseman for four seasons (1956 to 1959), he led the AL in 1957 in doubles and at-bats. He later managed the Twins, and when terminally ill Dick Howser retired during spring training, he took over the reins of the Royals. Name this player.

Q29 Before coming to Baltimore, this player led the AL in batting for the 1949 season, and prevented Ted Williams from winning the Triple Crown by .0001 (.3429 to .3428). Name him.

Q30 This first baseman has the distinction of being the first Oriole regular to hit over .300. Who is he?

Q31 How many separate stints did Dick Williams have with the O's?

BALTIMORE ORIOLES

A19 He was discovered playing second base in a church league.

A20 George Kell (Robinson backed up Kell for three seasons before taking over the job full-time in 1958.)

A21 Detroit's Hank Aguirre

A22 "Hoover"

A23 Oakland A's (The O's won the game 3–2 when Frank Robinson hit a 3-run homer in the bottom of the ninth.)

A24 Detroit's Aurelio Rodriguez

A25 One (He has the dubious distinction of playing on the most—15—All-Star losers. His lone win was on the 1962 team. One game, the 1961 contest, ended in a 1-1 tie.)

A26 Ty Cobb (3,033; Robinson does hold the major league record for most games played with one club.)

A27 Tommy Gastall (Ironically, the Boston College quarterback who Gastall succeeded, Harry Agganis, was signed by the Red Sox and died of leukemia in his second major league season.)

A28 Billy Gardner

A29 George Kell

A30 Bob Boyd (1957: .318)

A31 Three (1957, 1958, 1961)

THE UNIFORMS

Q32 At the age of 20, this ace became the youngest pitcher to start or win an All-Star Game. Who achieved this feat in 1959?

Q33 Milt Pappas spent nine of his 17 years in major league ball with the Orioles (1957–65). How many times did "Gimpy" have 10 or more wins in a season?

Q34 Milt Pappas was part of the famous trade that brought Frank Robinson to the Orioles in 1966. How many seasons after the trade did Pappas remain with the Reds?

Q35 Hoyt Wilhelm has the distinction of throwing the Orioles' first-ever no-hitter. In what year did he toss it?

Q36 In his 1958 debut, this player went 0-for-19, only to return to the O's in 1960 to win AL Rookie of the Year honors. His career was interrupted by a bad back and then with his service with the Marines during the Cuban missile crisis. Name this 6'3" shortstop.

Q37 This Oriole outfielder once played without shoes because he feared that lightning would strike his metal cleats. Who was he?

Q38 Since he couldn't break into the Dodgers' lineup, this first baseman was traded to the Orioles in 1960. The following year he set a record (since broken) with five grand slams in one season, including two straight in one game. Who is this onetime Bird?

Q39 Who gave Jim Gentile the nickname "Diamond Jim"?

Q40 Jim Gentile's American League single-season record of five grand slam homers, set in 1961, was surpassed in 1987 by what player?

Q41 What name appears on Boog Powell's birth certificate?

Q42 Before joining the O's in 1961, Boog Powell led the International League in homers. For what team was Powell at the top of the dinger derby?

Q43 What position did Powell play when he first arrived on the Orioles scene in 1961?

Q44 After being traded in February 1975, Boog Powell played three more years with two clubs. Name the teams he joined.

Q45 Onetime Oriole Chuck Essegian is one of the two players to ever swat two pinch-hit homers during a World Series. (He did it while playing for the Dodgers in the 1959 Series.) Who is the only other player to do this?

BALTIMORE ORIOLES

A32   Jerry Walker

A33   14

A34   Two and a half (He was traded to the Braves in a mid-1968 deal.)

A35   1958 (In his first season with the club, he threw the no-no on September 20 against the Yankees.)

A36   Ron Hansen

A37   Willie Tasby

A38   Jim Gentile

A39   Dodger Roy Campanella (The L.A. catcher tagged him with the moniker because he recognized the young slugger as "a diamond in the rough.")

A40   Yankee Don Mattingly, with six

A41   John Wesley Powell

A42   Rochester Red Wings (32)

A43   Left field (He was moved to first base in 1965.)

A44   Cleveland Indians (1975–76)
           L.A. Dodgers (1977)

A45   Bernie Carbo (1975; for the Boston Red Sox)

Q46   Ted Williams's "The Science of Hitting" was written by this former Oriole. His 11-year batting average was only .255, but he went on to become a highly regarded batting coach. Name him.

Q47   What club signed Whitey Herzog out of high school?

Q48   Identify the southpaw who was acquired by the Angels from the Baltimore organization in the 1961 draft and who then tossed the first major league no-hitter on the West Coast, against the Orioles on May 5, 1962.

Q49   This player earned the reputation for being "the greatest leadoff man in the world" by grounding into a double play only 33 times in 4,552 at-bats. He scored 99 runs three times in his Baltimore career, leading the American League in the 1971 season. Name him.

Q50   In the year that he was acquired, Luis Aparicio set an American League record while playing for Baltimore. What record did he establish?

Q51   When Luis Aparicio was dealt back to the White Sox after the 1967 season, the Orioles inserted his roommate into the shortstop spot. Identify Aparicio's replacement.

Q52   In his 18-year career, Luis Aparicio set a major league record by playing 2,581 games at shortstop. Whose mark did he surpass?

Q53   Luis Aparicio christened his son Nelson. For whom is he named?

Q54   Who has the distinction of being the modern-day Orioles' first 20-game winner?

Q55   What group of Orioles was called the "Baby Birds"?

Q56   In 1965, Curt "Clank" Blefary hit .260 with 22 homers and 70 RBIs. How did he earn his nickname?

Q57   Name the Oriole starting catcher who was forced to retire in 1965 due to a brain tumor.

Q58   Davey Johnson was traded to the Braves after the 1972 season, and the 1973 Braves became the only team in major league history to have three 40-home-run players. Besides Johnson, what other batters hit 40-plus dingers?

Q59   The first season after being traded, Davey Johnson hit .270 and had career highs of 43 home runs, 99 RBIs, 84 runs, and 81 walks. He was also named *The Sporting News*'s Comeback Player of the Year. Why did Earl Weaver trade Johnson away?

BALTIMORE ORIOLES

A46 Charlie Lau

A47 New York Yankees

A48 Bo Belinsky

A49 Don Buford

A50 Aparicio set an AL single-season record for fielding percentage by a shortstop (.983).

A51 Mark Belanger

A52 Luke Appling

A53 Aparicio's Sox teammate, Nellie Fox

A54 Steve Barber (1963: 20–13)

A55 The term was used for a group of promising young pitchers in the 1960s.

A56 His teammates christened him "Clank" for his "iron glove."

A57 Dick Brown (He died in 1970.)

A58 Hank Aaron (40)
Darrell Evans (41)
(Johnson had 43.)

A59 Weaver knew that Johnson was bulking up for power, but was afraid he would lose defensive speed and range.

Q60   How many Gold Gloves did Jim Palmer win?

Q61   Jim Palmer entered the Orioles' rotation in 1966. Who did he replace in the regular rotation?

Q62   Against what club did Jim Palmer make his major league debut, on April 17, 1965?

Q63   Against what team did Jim Palmer win his first major league decision, on May 16, 1965?

Q64   Jim Palmer was the winner of the second game in the 1966 World Series. What major league record did he establish on October 6?

Q65   Jim Palmer's last career victory came in the third game of the 1983 World Series when he took the mound in relief. Who did he relieve in that contest?

Q66   Jim Palmer has one career no-hitter to his name. What team did he hold hitless at Memorial Stadium on August 13, 1969?

Q67   With his victory in the 1983 World Series, Jim Palmer became the first major league player to register World Series wins in three different decades. What pitcher took the defeat in Palmer's last win?

Q68   Jim Palmer's final game as an Oriole was on May 12, 1984, at Memorial Stadium. What team did he face that day?

Q69   When Jim Palmer retired, only one American League pitcher had more consecutive 20-win seasons. Who is he?

Q70   Jim Palmer never yielded a major league grand slam, but did give one up while pitching in the minors. Name the player who hit the 4-run homer off Palmer.

Q71   Jim Palmer is a three-time Cy Young Award winner. Name the only three pitchers to win as many or more than Palmer.

Q72   Jim Palmer won the Cy Young in 1973, 1975, and 1976. Who are the only other two pitchers to have won the honor in consecutive seasons?

Q73   Jim Palmer polled 92.6 percent of the total vote when he was elected to the Hall of Fame. Only two pitchers have ever received a higher percentage. Name them.

BALTIMORE ORIOLES

A60   Four (1976–79)

A61   Milt Pappas (Pappas was traded during the 1966 season.)

A62   The Red Sox at Boston (Palmer came in to relieve and did not have a decision in the Orioles' 12–9 loss.)

A63   New York Yankees (He relieved Dave McNally in the third inning with the Orioles trailing 2–4. He helped his own cause when he hit a 2-run homer in the fourth.)

A64   He became the youngest pitcher (20 years, 11 months) to win a complete-game World Series shutout.

A65   Mike Flanagan

A66   Oakland A's (He beat Chuck Dobson, 8–0.)

A67   Steve Carlton

A68   Oakland A's (Five days later, he was given his unconditional release.)

A69   Walter Johnson (Johnson had 12 straight 20-win seasons, while Palmer and Lefty Grove had eight.)

A70   Johnny Bench (Bench was playing for Buffalo, and Palmer pitched for Rochester in the International League.)

A71   Steve Carlton (four)
Tom Seaver (three)
Sandy Koufax (three)

A72   Sandy Koufax (1965 and 1966)
Denny McLain (1968 and 1969)

A73   Tom Seaver (98.8 percent)
Bob Feller (93.75 percent)
(Seaver's percentage was the highest ever recorded in the Hall of Fame's history.)

Q74   In two seasons with Baltimore (1966 and 1967), this reliever went 11–9 before being traded to Cleveland. His claim to fame was his great Donald Duck impersonation, rather than his pitching. Name him.

Q75   Before coming to Baltimore, this pitcher gave up Stan Musial's 3,000th hit in 1958. He won his first 12 Oriole decisions and figured prominently in the club's 1966 and 1970 World Series. Name him.

Q76   After this player refused to be sent down to the minors, the O's were forced to trade him to the Senators in 1967. Later in the same season, as he faced his former club for the first time, he belted a grand slam. Who is he?

Q77   Name the Baby Bird who hurled shutouts in his first two big league starts, September 15 and 20, 1966.

Q78   This pitcher made an auspicious debut in 1967 when he threw five no-hit innings in his first major league game. He went on to win his first four decisions before going on to a 5–9 record. Who was this flash in the pan?

Q79   After becoming a free agent in 1981, Mark Belanger left the O's and played his final season with another club. With whom did he sign?

Q80   What major league fielding record did Don Buford equal in a June 25, 1970, game against Boston at Fenway Park?

Q81   Don Buford left the Orioles after the 1972 season. Where did he go to play baseball?

Q82   Name the Oriole who won a Bronze Star in Vietnam.

Q83   Before signing up with the Havana Sugar Kings of the International League, Mike Cuellar threw a no-hitter in 1955, at age 18. For what team was Cuellar pitching?

Q84   With what player did Mike Cuellar share the American League Cy Young Award in 1969?

Q85   Bobby Grich was named *The Sporting News*'s Minor League Player of the Year in 1971. With what club was he playing at the time?

Q86   Bobby Grich gained recognition as one of the league's best all-around second basemen over 15 seasons. What position was he playing when he broke into the majors?

Q87   In 1975, Bobby Grich became the third player in major league history to have 900 or more chances at second base in three consecutive seasons. Who were the first two?

BALTIMORE ORIOLES

A74   Eddie Fisher

A75   Moe Drabowsky

A76   Mike Epstein

A77   Tom Phoebus

A78   Bill Dillman

A79   Los Angeles Dodgers

A80   He had two assists in one inning while playing the outfield.

A81   Japan (1973–76; he became known as the "greatest leadoff man in the world" in his new country.)

A82   Al Bumbry

A83   Cuban dictator Fulgencio Batista's army team

A84   Denny McLain

A85   Rochester Red Wings

A86   Shortstop (He moved to second base full-time in 1973, his third season in the big leagues.)

A87   Fresco Thompson (Phillies: 1927–29)
        Oscar Melillo (Cardinals: 1930–32)

••• FAST FACTS •••

WORLD SERIES LOWEST RECORDS SET BY THE 1966 L.A. DODGERS—
   2 Runs
   17 Total Hits
   33 Consecutive Scoreless Innings
   .142 Batting Average

Q88 Bobby Grich set a single-season major league fielding record for second basemen twice—1973 and 1985. Who broke the record in 1980, only to have Grich reclaim it five years later?

Q89 Besides the Orioles, for what five major league teams did Don Baylor play?

Q90 What major league mark of dubious distinction did Don Baylor set in a June 15, 1974, game against the White Sox?

Q91 What major league single-season record did Don Baylor establish in 1987?

Q92 On June 28, 1987, Don Baylor and opposing pitcher Rick Rhoden combined to establish a new major league career record. What mark was set that day?

Q93 Don Baylor played in three World Series with three different teams. Name the clubs he played with.

Q94 Merv Rettenmund, who led the AL champs in hitting in 1970 and 1971, was also a star halfback at Ball State. Although he opted for a baseball career, Rettenmund was drafted by an NFL franchise. Name the team.

Q95 Name the pitcher who beaned Paul Blair in a 1970 game, causing severe eye and facial injuries to "Motormouth."

Q96 How many Gold Gloves does Paul Blair have in his collection?

Q97 In 1971, the Orioles had four 20-game winners. Name the bullpen quartet.

Q98 Of the four Oriole pitchers who won 20 games during the 1971 season, how many repeated as a 20-game winner?

Q99 What is the only other club to have as many 20-game winners in a season as the Orioles did in 1971?

Q100 On their 1973 roster, the Orioles had the American League Rookie of the Year as well as the runner-up. Identify the dynamic duo.

Q101 In 1973, the Orioles' trio of catchers combined for 103 RBIs—the most ever at that position in team history. Name the three backstops who contributed.

Q102 Why did the Reds trade Ross Grimsley to the Orioles in 1974?

Q103 With what two clubs did Ken Singleton play prior to arriving in Baltimore in 1975?

BALTIMORE ORIOLES

A88   Twin Rob Wilfong (Grich's fielding percentages were .995 in 1973 and .997 in 1985.)

A89   Oakland A's (1976 and 1988)
California Angels (1977–82)
New York Yankees (1983–85)
Boston Red Sox (1986–87)
Minnesota Twins (1987)

A90   He was caught stealing twice in the same inning.

A91   He was hit 28 times by a pitch.

A92   Rick Rhoden hit Don Baylor with a pitch, marking the 244th time that the former Oriole was pegged.

A93   Boston (1986)
Minneapolis (1987)
Oakland (1988)

A94   Dallas Cowboys

A95   Ken Tatum (California)

A96   Eight (1967, 1969–75)

A97   Dave McNally (21–5)
Jim Palmer (20–9)
Mike Cuellar (20–9)
Pat Dobson (20–8)

A98   One (Jim Palmer)

A99   1920 Chicago White Sox

A100   Al Bumbry (winner)
Rich Coggins

A101   Earl Williams (65)
Andy Etchebarren (23)
Ellie Hendricks (15)

A102   Because he refused to conform to the Reds' short-hair policy.

A103   New York Mets (1970–71)
Montreal Expos (1972–74)

Q104   In 1979, Ken Singleton swatted 35 dingers as a switch-hitter. He is one of three major leaguers to hit 35 or more homers in a season from both sides of the plate. Who are the other two?

Q105   Ken Singleton developed an allergy that required him to use "special equipment" while playing baseball. What did his condition necessitate?

Q106   True or false—Lee May struck out more than 100 times in a season 10 times in his career.

Q107   Rick Dempsey is the Orioles' all-time durable catcher, with 1,223 games behind the Baltimore plate. Who held the club record before Dempsey?

Q108   What is Rick Dempsey's full given name?

Q109   With whom did Rick Dempsey share the Orioles' catching responsibilities when he came to Baltimore in mid-1976?

Q110   When Rick Dempsey returned from the disabled list on August 21, 1977, the Orioles needed to move someone from the active squad. Who voluntarily retired to create the roster spot for Dempsey?

Q111   Rick Dempsey left Baltimore in 1987 and signed as a free agent with what team?

Q112   True or false—in his lone season with Baltimore, Reggie Jackson led the Orioles in home runs.

Q113   True or false—Reggie Jackson was the second player to have a candy bar named after him (after "Baby Ruth" was named for Babe Ruth).

Q114   How many times did Reggie Jackson win or tie for the American League home-run championship?

Q115   Besides baseball, what do Scott McGregor and George Brett have in common?

Q116   What is Tippy Martinez's given name?

Q117   Eddie Murray's baseball team at L.A.'s Locke High School included five future major leaguers. Name the pros from his school.

Q118   After a mere six months in the minors, Eddie Murray made "the Show" in 1977. What departed player did the slugger replace in the Orioles' offense?

BALTIMORE ORIOLES

A104   Mickey Mantle
Howard Johnson

A105   Singleton was allergic to wool and could only wear double-knit uniforms.

A106   True

A107   Gus Triandos (784 games)

A108   John Rikard

A109   Dave Duncan

A110   Brooks Robinson

A111   Cleveland Indians

A112   True. His 27 dingers were two more than his closest teammate, Lee May.

A113   False. Jackson was the first player to have a candy bar named after him. (Baby Ruth was named after President Theodore Roosevelt's daughter, not the Bambino.)

A114   Four (1973: 32, while playing with Oakland
1975: 36, Oakland
1980: 41, New York
1982: 39, California)

A115   They both attended El Segundo High School in California.

A116   Felix Anthony

A117   Eddie Murray (Class of '73)
Darrell Jackson (Class of '73)
Ozzie Smith (Class of '73)
Gary Alexander (Class of '71)
Rich Murray (Class of '74; Eddie's brother)

A118   Reggie Jackson

Q6. In Jimmy Dykes's 21 years as manager, what was the highest standing that any of his clubs finished?

BALTIMORE ORIOLES

Q44. Frank Robinson tied a major league record when he belted 38 homers as a rookie in 1956. Whose mark did he equal?

Q56. In 1965, Curt "Clank" Blefary hit .260 with 22 homers and 70 RBIs. How did he earn his nickname?

Q18. Why is Duane Pillette's name in the Orioles' record books?

Q119 What was noteworthy about Eddie Murray's Rookie of the Year Award of 1977?

Q120 In 1981, Eddie Murray was one of four players to lead the American League in homers with 22. Name the three players who equaled his dinger total.

Q121 Eddie Murray hit at least one grand slam in each season from 1981 through 1986. This put him one year short of the major league record. Who holds the mark with slammers in seven consecutive years?

Q122 Eddie Murray has been selected as a starter in only one All-Star Game—1985. Who came in second to Murray as the starting first baseman that year?

Q123 Eddie Murray is 1-for-10 in the five All-Star appearances he has made (he has been selected seven times). Who is the only pitcher to give up a hit to Murray in the mid-season classic?

Q124 Eddie Murray has been a switch-hitter for the last 11 years. Is Murray naturally right-handed or left-handed?

Q125 Eddie Murray was the first major leaguer to hit homers from both sides of the plate in consecutive games (May 8 and 9, 1987). Against what team did he achieve this?

Q126 Eddie Murray ranks second on the switch-hitters' home-run list. Who is at the top of the heap?

Q127 From 1978–85, this Baltimore pitcher was the only big leaguer to finish with a winning record each season. Identify him.

Q128 Name the four members of the Oriole organization who went to Japan in the 1969 major league All-Star trip.

Q129 John Lowenstein played seven of his 16 major league years with the Orioles (1979–85). How did Baltimore acquire him?

Q130 Who was the Most Valuable Oriole from 1981 until 1985?

Q131 Cal Ripken won the American League MVP Award in 1983. Who was second in the balloting that season?

Q132 How many times did Cal Ripken garner the most votes in American League All-Star voting?

BALTIMORE ORIOLES

A119   Murray was the first player to win the award as a designated hitter.

A120   Tony Armas (Oakland)
Dwight Evans (Boston)
Bobby Grich (California)

A121   Vern Stephens

A122   Rod Carew

A123   Met rookie Dwight Gooden (1984; Murray hit a double.)

A124   Right-handed (Ironically, he has been a better southpaw in seven of his eleven seasons as a switch-hitter.)

A125   Chicago White Sox (at Comiskey Park)

A126   Mickey Mantle

A127   Scott McGregor

A128   Earl Weaver
Rick Dempsey
Ken Singleton
Dennis Martinez

A129   The Texas Rangers waived the utility man in 1978 after one season.

A130   Eddie Murray

A131   Eddie Murray

A132   Two (1985, 1986)

Q133 When Ripken signed his $32 million contract in 1992, he was in the midst of his worst career drought. How many consecutive games had Ripken gone without a home run on the day he signed the pact (August 24)?

Q134 His sophomore season was no jinx for ace Mike Boddicker. In what two categories did he lead the American League that season?

Q135 In his rookie year, Fred Lynn led the American League in three categories. What were they?

Q136 Name the pair of pitchers who were the only two players to last the whole 1987 season on the Oriole roster.

Q137 Who was the only Oriole pitcher with a winning record in both 1987 and 1988?

Q138 Ray Knight's wife is a star in her own right. Who is she?

Q139 This Oriole ace had an auspicious debut in 1988, when he set a big league rookie record with 27 saves and earned Rookie of the Year honors. Name the freshman phenom.

Q140 Mike Devereaux attended Kelly Walsh High School in Wyoming. What other pro baseball player attended the school?

Q141 What club originally chose Mike Devereaux in the fifth round of the June 1985 Amateur Draft?

Q142 What organization drafted Glenn Davis in the 32nd round of the June 1979 free agent draft?

Q143 On September 24, 1992, Dave Winfield became the oldest player to reach the 100-RBI mark in a season. On that evening, the 40-year-old Winfield drove in four runs against the Orioles. Against what pitcher did the Blue Jay achieve his unique status?

Q144 The White Sox retired Harold Baines's uniform number after the club traded him to Texas. Only two players had previously had their numbers retired while they were still active in the major leagues. Who are they?

Q145 In 1992, 23-year-old Mike Mussina became the youngest Oriole hurler to make the All-Star squad since this 22-year-old did so in 1960. Who was he?

BALTIMORE ORIOLES

A133   55

A134   Wins (20)
ERA (2.79)

A135   Doubles (47)
Runs (103)
Slugging percentage (.566)

A136   Mike Boddicker
Eric Bell
(Each man had 10 wins.)

A137   Dave Schmidt

A138   Nancy Lopez (golf star)

A139   Gregg Olson

A140   Tom Browning

A141   Los Angeles Dodgers

A142   Orioles (Davis refused to sign with the club because he thought the bonus was too paltry.)

A143   Ben McDonald

A144   Frank Robinson
Phil Niekro

A145   Chuck Estrada

Q146   Match the Oriole with his retired number.
  (A)   Eddie Murray   4
  (B)   Jim Palmer   5
  (C)   Brooks Robinson   20
  (D)   Frank Robinson   22
  (E)   Earl Weaver   33

FYI

Q1   The 1954 franchise move from St. Louis to Baltimore was the first intercity shift of an American League club in 52 years. What was the last AL franchise to switch cities?

Q2   The Oriole franchise moved from St. Louis to Baltimore in 1954. Where was the franchise originally located?

Q3   As a sports editor for the *Baltimore News-Post*, this man led the campaign to lure major league ball back to Baltimore. Who was he?

Q4   Who did the Orioles meet in their first season opener, on April 15, 1954?

Q5   Identify the Oriole who pitched a complete game and won the first game played at Memorial Stadium.

Q6   The first pitch thrown at Memorial Stadium was hit for a single. Who hit it?

Q7   The first run scored at Memorial Stadium was a third-inning dinger on April 15, 1954. Who swatted the four-bagger?

Q8   Who is the only visiting player to hit an inside-the-park homer at Memorial Stadium?

Q9   Memorial Stadium saw 1,706 Baltimore regular-season victories against 1,321 losses. How many tie games were played at the facility?

Q10   Who hit the longest measured home run in Memorial Stadium history?

Q11   Originally, Memorial Stadium's dead center field was 450 feet from home plate. How many times was the distance contracted to its ultimate length of 405 feet?

Q12   Who was the last Oriole pitcher to win a game at Memorial Stadium?

BALTIMORE ORIOLES

A146   (A) Murray—33
               (B) Palmer—22
               (C) B. Robinson—5
               (D) F. Robinson—20
               (E) Weaver—4

A1   The Baltimore Orioles moved to New York and became the Highlanders in 1902. (Eventually, the team became the Yankees.)

A2   Milwaukee (The club moved to St. Louis in 1902.)

A3   Rodger Pippen

A4   Chicago White Sox (Baltimore won 3–1.)

A5   Bob Turley

A6   Chico Carrasquel (April 15, 1954: for the White Sox)

A7   Oriole Clint Courtney (off Chicago's Virgil Trucks)

A8   Detroit's Bill Tuttle (June 18, 1955: off Jim McDonald)

A9   Nine

A10   Twin Harmon Killebrew (May 24, 1964: off Milt Pappas; 471 feet)

A11   Four times (1956, 1959, 1962, and 1976)

A12   Jim Poole (October 5, 1991: vs. Detroit's Mark Leiter, 7–3.)

Q13   The last game in Memorial Stadium took place on October 6, 1991. The result was an Oriole loss to the Tigers, 7–1. Who made the last out in the ballpark?

Q14   Though the Orioles' inaugural season was tainted by a 54–100 record, they were not the cellar-dwellers. Who finished below the fledgling franchise?

Q15   The Orioles' dugout was originally on the first base side of Memorial Stadium. Why did the organization relocate it to the third base side in 1959?

Q16   The L.A. (California) Angels played the first game of their existence against the Orioles on opening day, 1961. Which Angel pitcher threw the complete-game victory over the O's?

Q17   Between 1969 and 1971, the Orioles became the third team in major league history to win 100 or more games for three consecutive seasons. Who were the first two clubs?

Q18   On May 28, 1969, in a game against Seattle, Earl Weaver's fifth-inning protest resulted in two runs being taken away from the Pilots and an eventual 9–5 win for the Orioles. What was the protest?

Q19   The Orioles forfeited a game on September 15, 1977, in Toronto when Earl Weaver pulled his team off the field four and a half innings into the contest. What caused the Oriole manager to pull his troops?

Q20   Since 1979, the Orioles have awarded the Clyde Kluttz Memorial Award annually to the Baltimore minor league player "who best exemplifies Clyde's integrity, desire, dedication, and loyalty" to the game and organization. Who is the only two-time winner of the honor?

Q21   The Orioles finished the 1986 season in last place, 22½ games out of first. How many games behind the leader were the O's on August 5 of that season?

Q22   The O's finished dead last in the American League in 1986 with a 73–89 record. When was the last time the club had landed in the AL cellar?

Q23   The 1988 Orioles are one of three teams in the annals of major league ball to have begun a season with a 1–16 record. What other clubs can claim that dubious distinction?

Q24   A pitcher who was on the Orioles' staff when they had their disastrous start in 1988 also played with another club that began the year with a 1–16 record. Who is he?

BALTIMORE ORIOLES

A13   Cal Ripken (Ripken hit into a 5–4–3 double-play.)

A14   Philadelphia Athletics (51–103)

A15   The team wanted to get out of the late-afternoon sun.

A16   Eli Grba

A17   Philadelphia Athletics (1929–31)
St. Louis Cardinals (1942–44)

A18   Seattle had batted out of turn. (Weaver waited until Seattle had scored to bring it to the attention of the officials.)

A19   Weaver wanted the tarpaulin removed from the Blue Jays' bullpen, claiming it was a hazard to his fielders. When umpire Marty Springstead refused, Earl removed his club. (The Orioles were losing 4–0 at the time.)

A20   Leo Gomez (1987 and 1990)

A21   Two and a half

A22   The Orioles had never finished last prior to 1986.

A23   Brooklyn Dodgers (1907)
Kansas City Royals (1992)

A24   Mike Boddicker (He pitched for the 1992 Royals.)

Q25   On May 15, 1991, the O's hosted the President and Mrs. Bush, and Queen Elizabeth II and Prince Philip. Who did Baltimore play that afternoon?

Q26   Channel 13 news reporter Kelly Saunders made Oriole and baseball history on June 13, 1992. What did she do on this date?

Q27   On June 21, 1992, the Orioles played a game that they later protested because the opponent's pitcher was suspected of scuffing the baseball with sandpaper. American League President Bobby Brown later denied the protest. Identify the pitcher who was suspected of cheating.

Q28   The incident in which manager Johnny Oates accused a Yankee pitcher of using a foreign substance (June 21, 1992) was not without its victims. What Oriole suffered a broken bone in his wrist due to a pitched scuffed ball that day?

Q29   The current site of center field at Camden Yards, 406 Conway Street, was the address of a famous Baltimore bar. Who owned the tavern at that site?

Q30   Opening day at Camden Yards was nearly perfect as the O's blanked Cleveland, 2–0, in just over two hours. What Baltimore ace defeated the Indians on that auspicious occasion?

Q31   In the "If you build it, they will come" category, Camden Yards was a tremendous hit in its first year of existence. Of the 80 home games of 1992, how many were sellouts?

SETTING THE STANDARD

Q1   Who was the first Oriole to average over .300 for a season?

Q2   Who was the first Oriole to win the club's Triple Crown (leading the team in batting average, homers, and RBIs in one season)?

Q3   Only two Orioles have ever hit for the cycle. Name them.

Q4   Cal Ripken holds the Orioles' "iron man" record for consecutive games played. Who held the record prior to Ripken?

BALTIMORE ORIOLES

A25   Oakland (The A's won 6–3)

A26   She was the second woman in history to handle the P.A. chores at a major league game.

A27   Yankee Tim Leary (Television replay clearly showed Leary putting something in his mouth and later removing something when he reached the dugout. The umpires questioned Leary during the game, but he refused to open his mouth, circumventing a possible suspension for the New Yorker.)

A28   Chris Hoiles

A29   Babe Ruth's father, George. (Ruth's Cafe was located on the ground floor of the family residence.)

A30   Rick Sutcliffe (April 6, 1992)

A31   67 (including 59 in a row)

---·---

A1   Bob Nieman (1956: .322)

A2   Gus Triandos (1955: .277 average, 21 homers, 65 RBIs)

A3   Brooks Robinson (July 15, 1960: vs. Chicago)
Cal Ripken (May 6, 1984: vs. Texas)

A4   Brooks Robinson (463 games)

SETTING THE STANDARD

Q5 On June 4, 1988, the Orioles played the longest game in their history. The five-hour, 46-minute game ended at 1:22 A.M. (the latest game ever at Memorial Stadium) with an Oriole 7–6 victory. Who did Baltimore defeat in 14 innings?

Q6 In this longest of Oriole games, Baltimore scored three runs in the bottom of the 14th inning to pull out a 7–6 win. All three runs came with two outs against the O's, and were the result of a player's throwing error. Who "threw the game away" in Baltimore's favor?

Q7 Two Orioles have hit safely in 22 consecutive games, the longest string in Baltimore history. Who are they?

Q8 Who holds the Orioles' single-season batting average record?

Q9 Name the Oriole who set a club record when he swatted 25 home runs in one season.

Q10 Who is the only Oriole to hit a home run in his first major league plate appearance?

Q11 Eddie Murray is the Orioles' all-time home-run leader, with 333. Who held the club mark previous to Murray?

Q12 Whose major league record for consecutive 20-homer seasons by a shortstop did Cal Ripken shatter in 1989?

Q13 Who swatted the most home runs for the O's in a season?

Q14 Three Orioles are in the 20-20 club (20 homers and 20 stolen bases in the same season). Who are they?

Q15 Jim Palmer leads all Oriole pitchers in career strikeouts (2,212), games (558), win (268), losses (152), innings pitched (3,947.2), and shutouts (53). What Baltimore pitcher has the lowest ERA (minimum: 500 innings)?

Q16 Who has the best win-loss percentage among all Oriole pitchers (minimum: 50 decisions)?

Q17 Which Oriole ace led the team in saves five times and saved at least 10 games each year from 1980 to 1984, with a career-best 21 in 1983?

Q18 Name the right-hander who hurled 36 consecutive shutout innings in 1961, setting the club record in the process.

Q19 Name the reliable Baltimore infielder who set major league records with 89 consecutive games and 458 chances without an error.

BALTIMORE ORIOLES

A5   New York Yankees

A6   Mike Pagliarulo

A7   Eddie Murray
Doug DeCinces

A8   Ken Singleton (1977: .328)

A9   Lee May (1978)

A10   Leslie "Buster" Narum (The pitcher entered the game in relief on May 3, 1963. Hitting for starter Chuck Estrada, he hit a homer at Detroit in his first and only at-bat in a Baltimore uniform.)

A11   Boog Powell (303)

A12   Ernie Banks's (Banks had eight.)

A13   Frank Robinson (1966: 49)

A14   Paul Blair (1969: 26 HRs, 20 SBs)
Don Baylor (1975: 25 HRs, 32 SBs)
Reggie Jackson (1976: 27 HRs, 28 SBs)

A15   Stu Miller (1963–67: 2.37)

A16   Steve Stone (40–21; .656)

A17   Tippy Martinez

A18   Hal Brown

A19   Jerry Adair (July 22, 1964 through May 6, 1965)

SETTING THE STANDARD

Q20   In 1992, Brady Anderson set a club single-season record for RBIs by a leadoff hitter. Whose record did he surpass?

Q21   Who holds the club single-season record for RBIs?

Q22   In 1980, Eddie Murray and Ken Singleton became only the second pair of switch-hitting teammates in 50 years to drive in 100 runs each in the same season. Who was the other duo to achieve this in the past half century?

Q23   The 1992 edition of the O's duplicated a dubious scoring record that was set 38 years earlier. What was that mark?

Q24   What Oriole struck out 160 times in one season, setting the club record?

GLORY DAYS

Q1   The Orioles were involved in the first World Series game ever played on an artificial surface. Who was the opponent and what stadium hosted that first fall classic?

Q2   The O's played in the first night game in World Series history. Who was their opponent and where was it played?

Q3   Reggie Jackson's 20 career RBIs in the World Series is second on the all-time list. Who is first?

Q4   Name the ex-marine who guided the Orioles to their first World Series victory, in 1966.

Q5   What was noteworthy about Jim Palmer's World Series shutout of October 6, 1966, against the Koufax-led Dodgers?

Q6   Whose 430-foot dinger in Game 3 of the 1966 World Series boosted the O's to a 1–0 win over the Dodgers?

Q7   Who set a World Series pitching record in 1966 with six consecutive strikeouts?

BALTIMORE ORIOLES

A20   Don Buford's (1970: 66)

A21   Jim Gentile (1961: 141)

A22   Reggie Smith and Ted Simmons (1974: St. Louis Cardinals)

A23   The team failed to score more than four runs for 21 straight games.

A24   Mickey Tettleton (1990)

————————————— · —————————————

A1   Cincinnati Reds
Riverfront Stadium (which opened in 1970, the same year that the Orioles and Reds played in the Series)

A2   Pittsburgh Pirates at Three Rivers Stadium (1971 Series)

A3   Steve Garvey (21)

A4   Hank Bauer

A5   Palmer was the youngest pitcher (20 years, 11 months) to win a complete-game shutout in the Series.

A6   Paul Blair's

A7   Moe Drabowsky

Q8   Los Angeles scored its last run of the 1966 World Series in the third inning of the first game. Who was the last Dodger to cross home plate?

Q9   Name the Oriole pitcher who equaled a Series record by striking out six consecutive Dodgers in the fourth and fifth innings of the first game in the 1966 fall classic.

Q10   What two Orioles hit consecutive home runs in the first inning of the initial game in the 1966 World Series?

Q11   Baltimore's starter in the first game of the 1966 World Series lasted only two and a third innings after giving up two runs, two hits, and five walks. Remarkably, he shut out the Dodgers to win the final game of the Series. Name him.

Q12   Going into the fifth inning of Game 2, the clubs were scoreless. Name the Dodger who misjudged back-to-back fly balls and had a throwing error in the same inning to give Baltimore three unearned runs.

Q13   Game 2 of the 1966 World Series was the last game that Sandy Koufax would ever play in. (An injured elbow forced him to announce his retirement at age 30 in mid-November.) Who was the last Oriole to face the Hall of Famer?

Q14   The first World Series game ever played in Baltimore was Game 3 in 1966. The Orioles won that contest 1–0. Whose homer defeated the Dodgers and ruined the 3-hitter pitched by L.A.'s Claude Osteen?

Q15   Name the two pitchers who faced each other in the fourth game of the 1966 World Series and gave up four hits apiece.

Q16   Like the third game of the 1966 Series, Game 4 was decided by one hit—a Baltimore home run. Name the Oriole who belted the fourth-inning dinger into the left-field stands.

Q17   What unlikely hitter belted a home run in the first American League Championship Series game ever played?

Q18   Who hit the first home run in American League Championship Series history?

Q19   Who scored the first run in American League Championship Series history?

BALTIMORE ORIOLES

A8   Lou Johnson (following a bases-loaded walk to Jim Gilliam)

A9   Reliever Moe Drabowsky

A10   Frank Robinson (two-run homer)
Brooks Robinson

A11   Dave McNally

A12   Center fielder Willie Davis

A13   Andy Etchebarren (Etchebarren grounded into a double play.)

A14   Paul Blair

A15   Baltimore: Dave McNally
Los Angeles: Don Drysdale

A16   Frank Robinson

A17   Mark Belanger (October 4, 1969: Orioles vs. Minnesota)

A18   Frank Robinson (October 4, 1969: off Twin Jim Perry)

A19   Frank Robinson (October 4, 1969)

*** FAST FACTS ***

The day that Cal Ripken inked what was then the most lucrative deal in baseball history (August 24, 1992), he also celebrated his 32nd birthday.

The Orioles won 10 of their first 11 games at Camden Yards, the best-ever start by a team in a new stadium.

Al Bumbry won a Bronze Star in the Vietnam War.

During the 1967 and 1968 seasons, Jim Palmer suffered career-threatening arm, shoulder, and back problems. The injuries were so severe that the Orioles left him unprotected in the draft, but no other team wanted to take a chance on him. After surgery and a stint in the minors, he fully recovered.

Q20 The first game of the 1969 AL Championship Series went into the 12th inning before Baltimore prevailed. The winning run was scored on a suicide squeeze play. Who laid down the bunt and who crossed home plate for the Oriole victory?

Q21 Who was the Minnesota Twin pitcher who held the Orioles to no runs and seven hits in 10²/₃ innings in Game 2 of the 1969 ALCS?

Q22 Dave McNally pitched an 11-inning shutout in Game 2 of the 1969 AL Championship Series. How many hits did he give up in the contest?

Q23 Who scored the lone run in Baltimore's 12-inning victory in Game 2 of the 1969 ALCS?

Q24 In the third game of the 1969 ALCS, the O's destroyed the Twins, 11–2. Who was the only Oriole to not hit safely in the game?

Q25 Though Baltimore struck for 11 runs in Game 3 of the 1969 ALCS, only one Oriole hit a home run. Who hit it?

Q26 Who was the Oriole leadoff batter who slammed the second pitch of the first game in the 1969 World Series for a home run?

Q27 Game 3 of the 1969 Series was decided by one Met—he hit a first-inning homer, made a backhanded running catch in the fourth inning to stop two runs from scoring, and, with the bases loaded and two down, made a headlong dive to prevent a Baltimore rally. Who shot the Birds down?

Q28 With the bases loaded and two down in the seventh inning of Game 3, this Oriole hit a shot up the alley in right-center that would have scored at least two runs. Name the Baltimore batter who had his hit stolen by this great Met play by Tommie Agee.

Q29 Earl Weaver was ejected from the fourth game of the 1969 World Series (by Shag Crawford). He became the third manager to be thrown out of a fall classic game. Who were the first two to be so "honored"?

Q30 The fourth game of the 1969 Series went ten innings with the score tied 1–1. What Oriole reliever's errant throw on a bunt allowed the Met winning run to score?

Q31 Who was the only Oriole pitcher to register a victory in the 1969 Series?

Q32 On September 17, 1970, the Birds clinched the division title when Boston eliminated New York. Where were the Orioles when they got the news?

BALTIMORE ORIOLES

A20   Paul Blair bunted.
Mark Belanger scored from third base.

A21   David Boswell

A22   Three (He didn't give up a hit after the fourth inning.)

A23   Boog Powell (from second base on pinch hitter Curt Motton's single)

A24   Jim Palmer (The pitcher went 0-for-5 as the team garnered 18 hits.)

A25   Paul Blair

A26   Don Buford (off Tom Seaver)

A27   Center fielder Tommie Agee

A28   Paul Blair

A29   1910: Cub manager Frank Chance (by umpire Tom Connolly)
1935: Cub manager Charlie Grimm (by umpire George Moriarty)

A30   Pete Richert's (on J. C. Martin's bunt)

A31   Mike Cuellar (Game 1: 4–1 victory on a 6-hitter)

A32   The team was on a bus to Washington for a night game at RFK.

Q33   The 1970 AL Championship Series only lasted three games, as the Orioles dominated the Twins. Of the 27 innings played, how many saw the Twins lead the Orioles?

Q34   Though staked to a 9–3 lead in the fifth inning, Mike Cueller was replaced in the first game of the 1970 American League Championship Series when he gave up three more runs. Who came on in relief and shut the Twins out in the last four and a half innings of the game?

Q35   In the third (and final) game of the 1970 AL Championship Series, Jim Palmer gave up only seven hits in his complete game to register a 6–1 win. Whose error cost Palmer the shutout?

Q36   What was noteworthy about pitcher Dave McNally's appearance in Game 3 of the 1970 World Series against the Reds?

Q37   Game 1 of the 1970 Series had one of the most controversial plays ever seen in postseason play. In the sixth inning, a Cincinnati batter chopped a ball in front of home plate that was fielded by the Oriole catcher. The catcher reached out and tagged the runner going home from third base with his empty glove. The home plate umpire mistakenly called the Red out because he was out of position to see that the mitt was empty. Name the three players (batter, catcher, and runner) on the play.

Q38   One of the great plays of any World Series took place in the second game of the 1970 Series when Brooks Robinson made a backhand stab at a ground ball that had passed him, fielded it, and, as he moved away from first base, threw the runner out at first. Who hit the grounder?

Q39   In the third game of the 1970 Series, Dave McNally helped his own cause as the Oriole hit a grand slam. This was his second homer in World Series play. Whose career record for pitchers did McNally tie when he belted his second fall classic dinger?

Q40   Who was the only Oriole pitcher to be "credited" with a loss in the 1970 World Series?

Q41   The 1971 Orioles had four pitchers on its staff with 20 or more wins. Who is the only one of that quartet to not make an appearance in the 1971 AL Championship Series?

Q42   Two of Baltimore's three starters in the 1971 ALCS went the distance. Name the only Oriole to be relieved in that Series and the pitcher who cleaned up after him.

BALTIMORE ORIOLES

A33 One (the first inning of the first game, the game was tied after two, and from that point on Baltimore led in every inning that was played.)

A34 Dick Hall (It was his only appearance in the ALCS that year.)

A35 Frank Robinson (He lost a Cesar Tovar fly ball in the sun, and Tovar later scored on a single by Leo Cardenas.)

A36 McNally became the first pitcher to crack a grand slam in a Series.

A37 Cincinnati pinch hitter Ty Cline hit the ball.
Oriole catcher Elrod Hendricks fielded the ball and tagged the runner with his empty glove.
Red Bernie Carbo was called out.
(The umpire on the call was Ken Burkhart.)

A38 Cincinnati's Lee May

A39 St. Louis's Bob Gibson

A40 Eddie Watt (Game 4: 1 inning pitched, 2 hits, 1 run, 9.00 ERA; Baltimore lost 6–5)

A41 Pat Dobson

A42 Dave McNally started Game 1, pitching seven innings, and Eddie Watt relieved.

Q43 Though Oakland held a two-run lead in the second inning of Game 1 in the AL Championship Series, the game turned around when a pitchout nabbed an opposing runner at third base. Whose rundown cost the A's momentum?

Q44 In Game 2 of the ALCS, Catfish Hunter gave up only seven hits to the Orioles, but four of them cleared the outfield wall. Whose two homers led Baltimore to their 5–1 win?

Q45 Whose 3-run homer in the first game of the 1971 Series brought the O's back from a 3–0 deficit and led them to a 5–3 win over Pittsburgh?

Q46 The sixth game of the 1971 Series went to the 10th inning tied 2–2. Who scored for Baltimore to give the Orioles the game?

Q47 The Orioles could only manage one run in the seventh game of the 1971 Series. Who was the lone Bird to cross home in the 2–1 loss?

Q48 Oakland ace Vida Blue opened for the A's in Game 1 of the 1973 ALCS. How long did he last before the O's knocked him off the mound?

Q49 The A's defeated the Orioles in Game 2 of the 1973 ALCS. How many consecutive playoff games had Baltimore won in championship series to that point?

Q50 In Game 3 of the 1973 ALCS, the Orioles lost 2–1 in 11 innings. Name the two opposing pitchers who went the distance.

Q51 Whose home run was one of three hits garnered by the O's in that Game 3?

Q52 The first man up for Oakland in the eleventh inning of the 1973 ALCS third game hit a homer to left field to win the game. Name him.

Q53 The Birds fell behind 4–0 in Game 4 of the 1973 ALCS until they registered four runs of their own in the seventh inning. Whose homer in the eighth inning gave Baltimore the 5–4 win?

Q54 Who swatted a Baltimore home run in the first inning of Game 1 in the 1974 ALCS against Oakland?

Q55 Whose homer in the third game of the 1974 AL Championship Series accounted for the only score by either team?

Q56 The Baltimore pitcher who lost the fourth and final game of the 1974 ALCS did not give up a hit through four and two-thirds innings, but walked nine batters, including the winning run. Whose no-hitter was a no-winner?

BALTIMORE ORIOLES

A43   Dave Duncan

A44   Boog Powell (Brooks Robinson and Elrod Hendricks swatted the other two dingers.)

A45   Merv Rettenmund

A46   Frank Robinson (He scored from third on Brooks Robinson's shallow fly to center field.)

A47   Elrod Hendricks (on an RBI single by Don Buford)

A48   Two-thirds of an inning. (Baltimore scored four runs on three hits and two walks.)

A49   10

A50   Baltimore: Mike Cuellar
Oakland: Ken Holtzman

A51   Earl Williams's

A52   Bert Campaneris

A53   Bobby Grich

A54   Paul Blair

A55   Sal Bando (Oakland won 1–0.)

A56   Mike Cuellar

Q57 How many hits did the Oakland A's get in the fourth game of the 1974 AL Championship Series?

Q58 Game 1 of the 1979 ALCS went to the bottom of the tenth inning tied at 3–3. Whose 3-run homer won the game for Baltimore?

Q59 After taking a one-game lead in the 1979 Series, the Pirates won the second matchup with a 3–2 come-from-behind victory. Whose ninth-inning pinch single was the difference for Pittsburgh?

Q60 The O's won the third game of the 1979 Series, 8–4. Name the Baltimore player who totaled four RBIs on two singles, a double, and a triple.

Q61 With the 1979 Series going to seven games, the Orioles drew first blood with a bases-empty homer in the third inning. Who gave the O's their first and only run in that contest?

Q62 Mike Boddicker tied a championship series record in the 1983 ALCS when he struck out 14 White Sox batters in Game 2. Whose marks did he equal?

Q63 Baltimore defeated Chicago 11–1 in Game 3 of the 1983 ALCS. Whose three-run homer in the first inning sparked the Oriole win?

Q64 What two Oriole pitchers combined to shut out the White Sox in Game 4 of the 1983 AL Championship Series?

Q65 Who was the 1983 Series MVP?

Q66 In the first game of the 1983 Series, the second Oriole at the plate knocked the ball out of the park to give Baltimore a 1–0 lead. Who put the O's ahead early?

Q67 After falling behind 2–0 in the third game of the 1983 Series, Baltimore fought back to score one in the sixth inning and two in the seventh. What Oriole scored the winning run on a Phillie error?

Q68 Tito Landrum, who played less than a quarter of the season with Baltimore, had a game-winning homer for the Orioles in the tenth inning of Game 4 in the 1983 AL Championship Series. Who did Landrum replace in the starting lineup?

Q69 Whose three hits and three RBIs led the Orioles to a 5–4 win in the fourth game of the 1983 World Series?

Q70 Who pitched a shutout in the fifth and final game of the 1983 Series for the Orioles?

BALTIMORE ORIOLES

A57   One (Their lone hit was a double by Reggie Jackson, but Oakland won 2–1.)

A58   John Lowenstein

A59   Manny Sanguillen

A60   Kiko Garcia

A61   Rich Dauer (Baltimore lost the game 4–1.)

A62   Detroit's Joe Coleman (1972: vs. Oakland)
Pittsburgh's John Candelaria (1975: vs. Cincinnati)

A63   Eddie Murray's

A64   Storm Davis
Tippy Martinez

A65   Rick Dempsey

A66   Jim Dwyer

A67   Benny Ayala (Phils shortstop Ivan Dejesus booted a grounder hit by Dan Ford to allow the Orioles' third run.)

A68   Rich Dauer's

A69   Dan Ford (The O's won 3–0.)

A70   Scott McGregor (He pitched a 5-hitter, striking out six and walking two.)

TRADES, WAIVES, AND ACQUISITIONS

Q1   The largest trade in major league history was executed in two parts in 1954. What two teams were involved in the deal?

Q2   How many players were exchanged in the two-part trade?

Q3   The Orioles gave up pitcher Mike Fornieles in 1957 for an infielder who had led all AL second basemen in errors the previous season and started the '57 season with a .063 batting average. Name this single-season Oriole.

Q4   What Hall of Famer was shipped to the White Sox in the 1963 swap that brought Luis Aparicio to the O's?

Q5   The best "one-two" draft choices in the Orioles' history took place during the 1961 June draft. Name Baltimore's premium picks.

Q6   Who was the Oriole traded to Kansas City in 1963 for Norm Siebern?

Q7   There were a total of four players involved in the 1965 trade that brought Frank Robinson from the Reds to the Orioles. Name them.

Q8   The first free agent draft was held in June, 1965. Who was the first player selected in the draft to make it to the Orioles?

Q9   The first free agent draft was held in 1965. Who was the first player to make it to Baltimore from that draft?

Q10 When Kansas City entered the league in 1968, it used its first pick in the expansion draft to select a player from the Baltimore organization. Name the Oriole lost to the Royals.

Q11 Who went to Houston in the 1968 trade that brought Mike Cuellar to the Orioles?

Q12 After shuffling him around the infield and outfield, the O's traded Curt Blefary in 1969 because of his defensive liabilities. Who did Houston send to Baltimore in the deal?

Q13 In a two-for-two swap, Rich Coggins and Dave McNally were sent north of the border to Montreal in 1974. Who came to play on the Chesapeake Bay?

Q14 Boog Powell and Don Hood were dispatched to the Indians before the 1975 season for a minor leaguer and this backstop. Who was the catcher?

BALTIMORE ORIOLES

A1   Baltimore Orioles
New York Yankees

A2   17

A3   Billy Goodman

A4   Hoyt Wilhelm

A5   Number one—Bobby Grich
Number two—Don Baylor

A6   Jim Gentile

A7   Frank Robinson came to Baltimore.
Milt Pappas, Jack Baldschun, and Dick Simpson went to Cincinnati.

A8   Pitcher Bill Dillman (The Orioles' 6th round pick from Wake Forest.)

A9   Right-handed pitcher Bill Dillman (Wake Forest—sixth-round pick)

A10   Pitcher Roger Nelson

A11   Curt Blefary

A12   Mike Cuellar

A13   Ken Singleton
Mike Torrez

A14   Dave Duncan

TRADES, WAIVES, AND ACQUISITIONS

Q15   Like the Royals in 1968, the Blue Jays used their first pick in the 1976 expansion draft to grab a Baltimore player. Who did the Orioles give up to Toronto?

Q16   During the 1976 season, the Orioles and the Yankees were involved in a five-for-five trade. Who were the ten players involved in the deal?

Q17   Used only as a stopper by the Birds, "Stan, The Man Unusual" was acquired in 1977 from Montreal with Joe Kerrigan and Gary Roenicke for Bryan Smith and Rudy May. Who is Stan, The Man Unusual?

Q18   In late 1985, the O's acquired Jackie Gutierrez from the Red Sox. Who went to Beantown in the even-up deal?

Q19   Though he led American League outfielders in errors in 1981, the Orioles acquired him the next season for Doug DeCinces. Name the former Minnesota Twin who came over in the trade.

Q20   Who did the Orioles give up in the deal that brought Wayne Gross to Baltimore after the 1983 season?

Q21   This right-hander, who made 61 appearances for the Birds as a rookie in 1987, came to Baltimore from San Diego with Terry Kennedy for Storm Davis. Who left the Left Coast and came to the O's in the deal?

Q22   Who did the Orioles deal away when they acquired Mike Morgan from the Seattle Mariners in 1987?

Q23   In a "pitcher perfect" trade, the Orioles shipped Mike Flanagan north of the border in a 1987 deal with Toronto. Who came to the O's?

Q24   Who came to Baltimore when the Orioles shipped Eddie Murray to the Dodgers in 1988?

Q25   Identify the Maryland native who came to the O's in a 1988 deal that sent Mike Boddicker to the Red Sox.

Q26   Who did the O's give up to acquire Glenn Davis from the Astros in January 1991?

BALTIMORE ORIOLES

A15 Infielder Bob Bailor (The first overall pick in the 1976 expansion draft was used by the Seattle Mariners to select Royal Ruppert Jones.)

A16 Baltimore sent Ken Holtzman, Doyle Alexander, Grant Jackson, Ellie Hendricks, and Jimmy Freeman to New York and obtained Dave Pagan, Rick Dempsey, Scott McGregor, Tippy Martinez, and Rudy May.

A17 Don Stanhouse

A18 Sammy Stewart

A19 Dan Ford

A20 Tim Stoddard

A21 Mark Williamson

A22 Ken Dixon

A23 Oswaldo Peraza

A24 Mike Devereaux

A25 Brady Anderson

A26 Pete Harnisch
Steve Finley
Curt Schilling

Washington Senators

THE SUITS

Q1   What Senator player-manager's signature appeared on all of the baseballs used in the American League for 14 years?

Q2   In what year was Clark Griffith named manager of the Washington club?

Q3   How did Clark Griffith earn the nickname "The Old Fox"?

Q4   As vice president of the League Protective Players' Association at the turn of the century, Clark Griffith instigated a players' strike against the National League that helped establish the American League in 1901. What was Griffith's "reward" for assisting the new league?

Q5   While managing the Reds, Clark Griffith broke down some of baseball's racial barriers. How did he do this?

Q6   What major strategic contribution did Clark Griffith make to professional baseball?

Q7   In 1946, Clark Griffith used a now-common instrument as a publicity stunt when Cleveland and Bob Feller came to Washington. What did "The Old Fox" introduce to baseball?

Q8   Identify the Hall of Famer who was Clark Griffith's son-in-law.

Q9   Nicknamed "Pinch," this Senator skipper was hit in the face by a ball and paralyzed on one side of his face. After suffering a nervous breakdown, he retired at the end of the season, but later coached for Ty Cobb. Who was he?

Q10   Ossie Bluege managed the Senators in 1922. What other position did he hold with the organization?

WASHINGTON SENATORS

A1   Joe Cronin's (As American League president from 1959 to 1972, his endorsement was carried on every ball.)

A2   1911 (October 30)

A3   During his pitching days, he utilized a six-pitch arsenal, including hiding the ball behind his body before delivering the toss. Lacking in skill, he used an assortment of spitballs, screwballs, and quick-pitch deliveries to register a career 240–144 record.

A4   He was named player-manager of the new AL Chicago franchise, the White Sox.

A5   He was the first to sign Cuban ballplayers.

A6   He developed the use of the relief pitcher.

A7   The radar gun. (The pregame show included a device borrowed from the U.S. Army to measure the speed of Feller's pitches.)

A8   Joe Cronin

A9   George McBride

A10   Comptroller (Bluege was an accountant.)

*** FAST FACTS ***

The world of professional sports was never far from veteran sports scribe's Bob Addie's life. Besides covering the Senators for 37 years with the *Washington Times-Herald* and the *Post*, he was married to Pauline Betz, four-time winner of the U.S. women's tennis crown.

HARMON KILLEBREWS' AWARDS:
MVP—1969
HOME RUN CROWN—1959, 1962–64, 1967, 1969
RBI CROWN—1962, 1969, 1971
ALL-STAR—1959, 1961, 1963–71
HALL OF FAME—1984

Q11   How old was Bucky Harris when he became the "Boy Manager" of the Senators in 1924?

Q12   How many separate tenures did Bucky Harris have as manager of the Senators?

Q13   Bucky Harris led the Senators to two American League pennants (1924 and 1925) and a world championship (1924). What other club did Harris take to the Series?

Q14   Besides managing the Senators, Bucky Harris served at the helm of four other teams. The players on one of those clubs threatened to strike when Harris was fired during the 1943 season. What organization almost saw its players walk out due to Bucky's release?

Q15   What other Hall of Famer came from Bucky Harris's hometown of Pittstown, Penn.?

Q16   While a player-manager with the Red Sox, Cronin pulled himself out of the regular lineup in 1942 to make room for an up-and-coming player. Who did he substitute for himself?

Q17   As league president, Joe Cronin fired two umpires for "incompetency" in 1970. What was the real reason behind the terminations?

Q18   Who was the last manager of the original Senators, in 1960, and the first manager of the Twins, in 1961?

Q19   Though he never played for the Senators, Gil Hodges was acquired by Washington in a trade on May 23, 1963. Who did the club give up to obtain the manager?

Q20   Gil Hodges was traded back to New York in 1967. Who did the Mets send to Washington in exchange?

Q21   Gil Hodges once held the NL mark for career grand slams, with 14. Name the two men who have since eclipsed his mark.

WASHINGTON SENATORS

A11   27 years old

A12   Three (1924–28
                 1935–42
                 1950–54)

A13   New York Yankees (The Yankees won the Series, in 1947.)

A14   Philadelphia Phillies

A15   Hughie Jennings

A16   Johnny Pesky

A17   Cronin discovered that the two were attempting to form a union for the umpires.

A18   Cookie Lavagetto

A19   Jimmy Piersall (to the New York Mets)

A20   Pitcher Bill Denehy (plus $100,000)

A21   Willie McCovey (18)
                 Hank Aaron (16)

Q1   Who was the last active Senator from the original franchise (1901–1960)?

Q2   A major leaguer from 1890 through 1907, this outfielder had the distinction of playing for three Washington clubs in three major leagues (American Association—1891; National League—1892; American League—1904). Name him.

Q3   Which Senator defied the odds and won a $500 bet when he caught a ball thrown from the top of the Washington Monument, a distance of 550 feet?

Q4   One of Walter Johnson's nicknames was "Barney." Where did it originate?

Q5   Who got the first hit ever given up by Walter Johnson in his big league career?

Q6   Against what club did Walter Johnson rack up the first of his 416 career victories?

Q7   In September 1908, Walter Johnson vaulted from local hero to national star when he pitched three shutouts against the New York Highlanders. Over how many days did Johnson thrice whitewash the pinstripers?

Q8   Walter Johnson set a major league record when he tossed a string of 56 scoreless innings during the 1913 season. What two players eventually surpassed Johnson's streak? (Hint: They were both Dodgers.)

Q9   Walter Johnson left the Senators after the 1914 season and signed a contract with another club in the newly formed Federal League. Name the team that signed the franchise player from Washington.

Q10   Though the 1916 Senators languished in seventh place, Walter Johnson went 25–20 with a 1.89 ERA. What ML record did he establish that year which still stands today?

Q11   In the same year that Walter Johnson won only eight games, he tossed the only no-hitter of his stellar career. When did that paradox occur?

Q12   Walter Johnson managed the Senators for four seasons (1928–32). What other big league club did he manage?

Q13   Who is the only pitcher to win more games than Walter Johnson?

Q14   Walter Johnson still holds the major league mark for victories in 1–0 games. How many of those wins did he have?

Q15   Besides holding the record for 1–0 wins, Johnson set the mark for 1–0 losses. How many games did he lose by that score?

WASHINGTON SENATORS

A1   Jim Kaat (1959–83)

A2   Patsy Donovan

A3   Gabby Street

A4   Barney Oldfield (Oldfield was a "mile-a-minute" race car driver of the day. The name stuck because of Johnson's fastball.)

A5   Detroit's Ty Cobb (August 2, 1907: Cobb hit a bunt single; Johnson lost the first game, 3–2.)

A6   Cleveland Blues (August 7, 1907: He won 7–2 over the club that would later become known as the Indians.)

A7   Four days

A8   Don Drysdale (1968: 58)
Orel Hershiser (1988: 59; Hershiser went on to pitch eight more scoreless innings in the playoffs.)

A9   Chicago Whales (Clark Griffith re-signed Johnson and returned the $6,000 bonus paid him to the Whales.)

A10   Johnson pitched 371 innings without giving up a home run.

A11   1920

A12   Cleveland (1933–35)

A13   Cy Young (Young won 511 to Johnson's 416.)

A14   38

A15   26

Q16   Walter Johnson set an American League record by registering 66 victories over one opponent. Who was his patsy?

Q17   Only two players ever hit two homers in one game against Walter Johnson. Who were they?

Q18   Walter Johnson lost 279 games in his career. What two ML pitchers lost more?

Q19   Nicknamed for a popular Spanish-American War song, this Senator pitcher had a lifetime record of 15–51. The epitome of his career was the game in which he lost a one-hitter when, after a two-out error, he walked seven consecutive batters on 3–2 counts. Name this early-century Senator.

Q20   This first baseman played six-plus years with the Senators before going to the Chicago White Sox in 1917. Known as a malcontent, he was later considered to be the ringleader of the 1919 World Series fix. Name the player who was eventually banned from baseball.

Q21   This Senator first baseman set AL career records for his position for games, putouts, double plays, and total chances (all have since been broken). He still holds the AL record among AL first basemen for leading or tying for the lead in fielding six times. Name him.

Q22   Hall of Famer Sam Rice was known for his abilities in the outfield, but when he came to the Senators in 1915, he played a different position. What was it?

Q23   In 1917, future Hall of Famer Eddie Plank was in his last season. Pitching for the St. Louis Browns, he held the Washington Senators hitless for eight and two-thirds innings one day. Name the batter, known as the best hit-and-run man of his day, who doubled to end Plank's bid.

Q24   Although pitcher Al Schacht played for just two years in the majors (1919–21), he attended 25 World Series and 18 All-Star Games. How was that possible?

Q25   Doc Ayers received special dispensation from the league in 1919—one of eight to receive such special consideration. What was granted to Ayers?

Q26   The only son of a state governor to play in the majors started his career with the 1919 Senators. Name the infielder who was nicknamed "The Governor."

WASHINGTON SENATORS

A16 Detroit

A17 Jack Fournier (1914: White Sox)
Lou Gehrig (1926: Yankees)

A18 Cy Young (315)
Pud Galvin (308)

A19 William "Dolly" Gray (The song he was named after was "Goodbye, Dolly Gray.")

A20 Chick Gandil

A21 Joe Judge

A22 Pitcher

A23 Eddie Foster

A24 Schacht was the "Clown Prince of Baseball," which enabled him to tour USO bases' ballparks with a mix of mime and anecdotes.

A25 The league allowed him to continue to throw a spitball after it was banned that season.

A26 Frank Ellerbe (His father was the governor of South Carolina.)

*** FAST FACTS ***

Hall of Famer Goose Goslin was responsible for the first fine ever levied against an umpire. In the 1935 World Series, the outfielder got into a heated argument with Bill Klem, the Hall of Fame umpire. When Klem used foul language, baseball Commissioner Kenesaw Landis fined Klem, but not Goslin.

Pitcher Monte Weaver had an impressive freshman season when he compiled a 22–10 record. After the season, he went on a strict vegetarian diet, and lost the zip off his fastball. He stumbled to a 10–5 mark in 1933, went to the minors, and finally ended his veggie diet. Weaver went back to the Senators in 1934 and pitched for them, without distinction, until 1939.

Q27 This outfielder finished a fairly undistinguished 11-year career with the Senators (1921). He does have the distinction of being the first major leaguer to ever pinch-hit for Babe Ruth, while playing for the Red Sox. Who is he?

Q28 Hall of Famer Goose Goslin played with the Senators for 11 1/2 years of his 18-year major league career. How many separate terms did he have with Washington?

Q29 Goose Goslin played for only three teams during his career. With what other clubs was he associated besides the Senators?

Q30 Goose Goslin won his only batting title in 1928. Going into the last day of the season, he was tied with a player whose team he was opposing that very day. Who did he edge out by going 2-for-4 that day?

Q31 This rookie was the Senators' only .300 hitter in 1922. Who was he?

Q32 Senator hurler Firpo Marberry is generally acknowledged as the first of his kind in baseball. For what was he known?

Q33 Hall of Famer Mickey Cochran's career was ended when this one-time Senator pitcher fractured his skull with a pitch in 1937. Who tossed the errant pitch?

Q34 Name the three Senators who made up an all-.300 outfield at the plate in 1928.

Q35 This Senator screwballer led the league in relief appearances (56) in 1927. The following season, he topped the AL with a 2.51 ERA. After retiring from the diamond, he joined the golf tour and won a number of senior titles. Who was he?

Q36 In 1928 and 1930, "Sad Sam" Jones was the leading pitcher for the Senators. What major league record does Jones share with four other players?

Q37 This Senator broke Hank Greenberg's wrist in 1935, constantly fought with other players, was suspended in 1938 because of racial slurs, and committed suicide in a D.C. police station while being questioned on bad-check charges. Who was he?

Q38 Lou Gehrig had great success against this southpaw. Nicknamed "Gimpy," he is on record for giving up the most home runs (15) to the "Iron Horse." Who is he?

WASHINGTON SENATORS

A27   Duffy Lewis

A28   Three (1921–mid-1930, 1933, and 1938)

A29   St. Louis Browns (1930–32)
Detroit Tigers (1934–37)

A30   St. Louis Brown Heinie Manush (Goslin went into his last at-bat ahead of Manush, and attempted to get himself thrown out of the game rather than go to bat. After failing to be ejected, he stepped up and got an infield hit to win the batting title.)

A31   Goose Goslin (.324; though Goslin played for the Senators in 1921, he only came to bat 50 times and still qualified as a rookie the following season.)

A32   Marberry was considered the first relief pitcher in the sport.

A33   Bump Hadley (Hadley was pitching for the Yankees at the time.)

A34   Sam Rice (.328)
Goose Goslin (.379)
Red Barnes (.302)

A35   Garland Braxton

A36   He spent 22 consecutive seasons pitching in one league. (He shares the record with Herb Pennock, Early Wynn, Red Ruffing, and Steve Carlton.)

A37   Jake Powell

A38   Lloyd Brown

THE UNIFORMS

Q39   On August 5, 1932, Detroit's Tommy Bridges was one out away from a perfect game in a 13–0 drubbing of the Senators. Whose pinch single spoiled the Tiger's perfection?

Q40   Known as "Prof," this right-hander had a master's degree in mathematics from Emory and Henry College in Virginia. In his rookie season of 1932, he went to the head of the class with a 22–10 record. Who was he?

Q41   This two-time All-Star (1938 and 1947) spent all 11 years of his major league career with Washington. The third baseman-outfielder batted over .300 four times, scored 100-plus runs four times, and led the AL in triples (16) in 1939. Name him.

Q42   Name the battery mates who were brothers and played for the Senators in the late 1930s and early 1940s.

Q43   This player, who later became the team's manager, performed in four separate decades and set a major league mark for most games played at first base. Who was he?

Q44   Lefty Gomez appeared in 368 games with the Yankees and the Senators over a 14-year span. How many of those games did he play for Washington?

Q45   After playing eight games with the Senators in 1944, this infielder never again saw major league baseball as a player, but did come back to manage for seven years. Twice in his managing career he pinch-hit for pitchers who had no-hitters going. Name him.

Q46   The 1945 Senators jumped from last place in the previous season to second, one and a half games behind pennant-winner Detroit. The primary reasons for the club's success were the four knuckleballers who made up the bullpen. Name the quartet of specialists.

Q47   As a wartime player in 1945, this right-hander won 14 games for the Senators. In the off-season, he worked in a slaughterhouse, where he killed cattle with a baseball bat. Who was he?

Q48   This Hall of Famer led the AL five times in passed balls, probably as a result of all the knuckleballers he caught. Who was he?

Q49   Finish this 1949 Senators' slogan: "We'll win plenty with _____!"

Q50   Name the two brothers who pitched at different times for the Senators and whose nicknames were "Big Potato" and "Little Potato."

WASHINGTON SENATORS

A39   Dave Harris's

A40   Monte Weaver

A41   Buddy Lewis

A42   Wes Ferrell (pitcher)
Rick Ferrell (catcher)

A43   Mickey Vernon

A44   One (After going 0–1 for Washington in 1943, he retired.)

A45   Preston Gomez (While managing for the Padres, he pinch-hit for Clay Kirby.
The Astros' Don Wilson was pulled from the game in favor of a pinch hitter
as well. Both had no-hitters going at the time.)

A46   Dutch Leonard (17–7)
Roger Wolff (20–10)
Mickey Haefner (16–14)
Johnny Niggeling (7–12)

A47   Marino Pieretti

A48   Rick Ferrell

A49   Dente (referring to infielder Sam Dente)

A50   Carlos "Big Potato" Pascual (1950)
Camilo "Little Potato" Pascual (1954–60, 1967–69)

Q51   How old was Harmon Killebrew when he was signed by the Senators in 1954?

Q52   For the first five years of his pro career, Harmon Killebrew was shuttled between the majors and the minors. In 1959, he became a regular when the starting second baseman went down with an injury. Who did "Killer" replace?

Q53   How many times during his career did Killebrew lead the league in homers?

Q54   Harmon Killebrew and his roommate were the first big leaguers to combine for two grand slams in one inning (July 18, 1962). Who was Harmon's talented roomie?

Q55   With what club did Harmon Killebrew end his playing career?

Q56   He was the first Senator to hit three consecutive home runs. In 1960, he finished second to Mickey Mantle for the AL home run title (40 to 38). Name him.

Q57   In 1958, this Senator had ten relief wins and 18 saves, accounting for 46 percent of the last-place Washington's victories. His 1.75 ERA was the best for the franchise since Walter Johnson's 1.49 in 1919. Who is he?

Q58   After leaving the Senators, this pitcher established a major league record by throwing in $84\frac{1}{3}$ consecutive innings without giving up a walk. Who was this former marine drill instructor?

Q59   This Senator became the first major leaguer to hit into a triple play on opening day when he achieved the dubious feat in 1959. Along with his six brothers, he barnstormed around the country on a basketball team. Name this player.

Q60   Nixon wasn't the first "Tricky Dick" to play games in Washington. The Senators had a right-handed pitcher who carried the same nickname and led the AL with a 2.40 ERA in the expansion club's inaugural season (1961). Name this player.

Q61   Who was the first pitcher to win a game at D.C. (now RFK) Stadium?

Q62   After being acquired in a trade in 1962, this Senator belted a home run in his major league debut to lead Washington to a 1–0 win over Chicago. After averaging one strikeout every four at-bats, he was traded to Philadelphia after five seasons. Name him.

WASHINGTON SENATORS

A51   18 years old

A52   Pete Runnels

A53   Six (1959, 1962, 1963, 1964, 1967, 1969)

A54   Bob Allison

A55   Kansas City Royals (1975)

A56   Jim Lemon

A57   Dick Hyde

A58   Bill Fischer

A59   Ed Fitz Gerald

A60   Dick Donovan

A61   Bennie Daniels

A62   Don Lock

*** FAST FACTS ***

After graduation from the University of Michigan, Pete Jablowski gave up a promising musical career and opted for a gig in professional baseball. The pianist and bandleader played under his real name from 1930 until 1933 and then had his last name legally changed to Appleton.

Pitcher Wes Ferrell's temper and arrogance were well known, accounting for the fact that he played for six teams in his 15-year major league career. He was once suspended by a team for refusing to be taken out of a game, and he walked out of one game without permission.

Bill Zuber, a right-handed pitcher who won a career-high nine games for the 1942 Senators, was the only Amish player in big league history.

Q6. Against what club did Walter Johnson rack up the first of his 416 career victories?

WASHINGTON SENATORS

Q19. Though he never played for the Senators, Gil Hodges was acquired by Washington in a trade on May 23, 1963. Who did the club give up to obtain the manager?

Q65. For what college was 6'8" Frank Howard an All-American in both baseball and basketball?

Q73. Why is pitcher Joe Coleman noteworthy in Senator history?

Q63 In a 1965 game, this Senator struck out eight of the first nine Tigers batters that he faced. His major league career lasted only four seasons. Name him.

Q64 By what two nicknames was Frank Howard known?

Q65 For what college was the 6'8" Frank Howard an All-American in both baseball and basketball?

Q66 In May 1968 Frank Howard set an ML record for home runs. How many dingers did Hondo hit in 20 at-bats?

Q67 Howard hit a career-high 48 dingers in 1969 but missed the home-run crown by one. Who edged him out for the title that year?

Q68 Frank Howard played on four teams between 1958 and 1973. Name them.

Q69 With what club did Frank Howard play his last professional baseball game?

Q70 What two teams did Frank Howard manage in the majors?

Q71 In how many seasons did Frank Howard lead the American League in home runs?

Q72 Dallas Green gained more renown as a major league manager than as a pitcher. Besides pitching for Washington in 1965, he appeared on the mound for the Phillies (1960–64, 1967) and the Mets (1966). Of his 42 career decisions, how many came with the Senators?

Q73 Why is pitcher Joe Coleman noteworthy in Senator history?

Q74 This backup catcher played all seven of his major league seasons (1965–71) with the Senators. His claim to fame wasn't his mediocre baseball career, but the fact that he had a horse named after him who competed in the 1971 Kentucky Derby and Belmont Stakes. Name this player.

Q75 In his rookie season with the Senators (1967), this sidearm specialist saved 12 games and had a 1.70 ETA. Baseball wasn't his only talent, though. His credentials included a Ph.D. and he worked as a zoologist and anthropologist. Who was this erudite athlete?

WASHINGTON SENATORS

A63   Jim Duckworth

A64   "Hondo"
"The Capital Punisher"

A65   Ohio State

A66   10 (in six consecutive games)

A67   Harmon Killebrew

A68   L.A. Dodgers (1958–1964)
Washington Senators (1971)
Texas Rangers (1972)
Detroit Tigers (1972–73)

A69   Taiheiyo (Howard went to Japan in 1974, but he hurt his back striking out in his first game and never played again.)

A70   San Diego Padres (1981)
New York Mets (1983)

A71   Two (1968 and 1970)

A72   None (All 42 decisions—for a 20–22 record—were with the Phillies, even though he pitched 14.1 innings for Washington and five for New York.)

A73   He was the first player selected by the team in the first-ever free agent draft (1965).

A74   Jim French

A75   Dave Baldwin

Q76 The Senators' primary shortstop in their last season of existence, he finished third in the AL record books with a .437 career on-base average after 17 seasons. Name him.

Q77 Who threw the last pitch for the Senators in 1971 before the franchise moved to Texas?

FYI

Q1 How long did the Senators call Washington home?

Q2 On March 29, 1905, a committee of Washington writers voted for a new nickname for the capital's team, but the fans held on to the "Senators" moniker. What was the writers' alternative?

Q3 The Senators hosted the first president to throw the pitch on an opening day. Who was the first chief executive to do this?

Q4 Bob Addie covered the Senator beat for 37 years with the *Washington Times-Herald* and the *Post*. His column also appeared in *The Sporting News*. By what name was his column known?

Q5 In the expansion Senators' 10 years in the district, how many winning seasons did the team chalk up?

Q6 Several of the center-field seats at RFK were painted different colors. Why was that done?

Q7 What was the team's motto in 1964?

Q8 In 1966, Joy Hawkins McCabe made baseball history at D.C. Stadium. What did she do?

WASHINGTON SENATORS

A76   Toby Harrah

A77   Joe Grzenda (Grzenda did not make the trip south with the team. In 1972, he ended up in St. Louis.)

---   ·   ---

A1   71 years (1901–1971)

A2   Nationals

A3   William Howard Taft (April 14, 1910)

A4   "Addie's Atoms"

A5   One (1969: 86–76; fourth place)

A6   The different colors represented the landing spots of some of Frank Howard's home runs.

A7   "Off the Floor in '64!"

A8   She was the first woman in history to be the public announcer at a major league baseball game.

---   ·   ---

Q1   Who was the Senator catcher who caught the entire 1942 game for the American League All-Stars?

Q2   As a Senator, Mickey Vernon led the AL in batting twice: in 1946 with a .353 average and in 1953 with a .337 mark. How old was the veteran when he topped the league in 1953?

Q3   On July 16, 1909, Washington was involved in the longest scoreless game in AL history. Who did it meet in that 0–0 18-inning contest?

Q4   Who was the American League Rookie of the Year in 1958?

Q5   Who holds the 1961–71 Senators' single-season records for saves, games pitched, and games finished?

Q6   Name the Senator who set a major league record in 1970 by losing 14 games in relief.

Q7   Name the Senators' pitcher who established a major league record (since tied) by losing 19 consecutive games.

Q8   An American League record established in 1901 still stands today—22 errors in a doubleheader by both teams. Who was Washington playing when the mark was established?

Q9   This Senator established an American League record in 1926 for most double plays started by an outfielder in a game (3). Name him.

Q10   This Senator set the record straight for Washington on several different occasions, leading the league in total chances per game (1967–69), double plays (1967), and putouts (1969). Who was he?

Q11   The Washington Senators totaled only 13 stolen bases for the season in 1957. Who led the club in steals?

Q12   Who set the standard for leading the big leagues in stolen bases five straight seasons?

WASHINGTON SENATORS

A1   Jake Early

A2   35 years old

A3   Detroit Tigers

A4   Senator Albie Pearson

A5   Ron Klein

A6   Darold Knowles

A7   Bob Groom (From June 19 through September 25, 1909; the rookie also tied the AL mark for losses that season with a 7–26 mark.)

A8   Cleveland (September 21, 1901: Washington won both games when the Blues, as Cleveland was originally named, committed 16 muffs in the twin bill.)

A9   Ira Flagstead

A10   Kem McMullen

A11   Julio Becquer, with three

A12   George Case (1939–43)

*** FAST FACTS ***

The Senators played host to the first Yankee team on April 10, 1913. The New York club changed its name that year from the Highlanders, but it didn't help the Big Apple team as Washington opened the season with a 2–1 victory, behind Walter Johnson's pitching.

Senator backstop Eddie Ainsmith stole second, third, and home in the ninth inning of a game played June 26, 1913, against the Athletics. All of Ainsmith's thefts were scored as stolen bases, even though each of them went unchallenged.

Q1 What Senator belted three homers in both the 1924 and 1925 World Series?

Q2 In 1924, with the score deadlocked 3–3 in the bottom of the 12th inning in Game 7, Washington scored the winning run after a New York catcher dropped a sure-out foul ball. Name the Giant backstop who gave new life and ultimately the Series to the Senators.

Q3 Name the Senator whose foul ball was dropped and who eventually scored the winning run in that seventh game of the 1924 World Series.

Q4 It was the "pebble hit" that drove in the game- and Series-winning run. Who was the Senator who is credited with the RBI and the Giant third baseman who saw the grounder leap over his head?

Q5 Who was the Senator shortstop who committed eight errors in the 1925 World Series?

Q6 The third game of the 1925 World Series contains one of the most provocative calls in World Series history. Behind by one run in the eighth inning, Pirate Earl Smith hit a long ball near the fence that caused a Senator to fall into the stands. When he appeared, he had the ball. Who was that center fielder?

Q7 With the score tied 6–6 in the top of the eighth inning, this Senator drilled a homer in the seventh game of the 1925 World Series. Name the player who gave Washington a 7–6 lead.

Q8 In losing the 1925 World Series, the Senators became the first team in World Series to achieve something. What distinction did the club earn?

Q9 This Senator made history as the first player thrown out of a World Series game, when he yanked an umpire's bow tie that was held in place with a rubber band, and then let it snap back. Who was this ornery player?

Q10 Who did the Senators face in the 1933 World Series?

Q11 Who was the only Senator pitcher to win a game in the 1933 Series?

Q12 The fifth and final game of the 1933 Series went ten innings with the score tied 3–3. Whose home run ended any hopes of a Washington comeback?

WASHINGTON SENATORS

A1   Goose Goslin

A2   Hank Gowdy (Gowdy tripped over his catcher's mask and dropped the easy foul ball. Instead of the Senators having two outs, they started a rally with only one out.)

A3   Harold "Muddy" Ruel

A4   Washington: Earl McNeely
New York: Fred Lindstrom

A5   Roger Peckinpaugh

A6   Sam Rice (Rice tumbled into the stands and 15 seconds later returned to the field with the ball in his glove. Though it was unclear whether he had caught the ball or picked it up in the confusion, umpire Cy Rigler called Smith out. Pittsburgh lost the protest—and the game, by one run.)

A7   Roger Peckinpaugh (The Pirates scored three in the bottom half of the inning to win, 9–7.)

A8   They were the first team to lose the Series after taking a 3–1 lead in a best-of-seven format.

A9   Heinie Manush

A10   New York Giants

A11   Earl Whitehill (Game 3: 4–0 shutout)

A12   Mel Ott's (off reliever Jack Russell)

TRADES, WAIVES, AND ACQUISITIONS

Q1 This All-Star pitcher came to Washington with Heinie Manush in exchange for Goose Goslin in a 1930 trade with St. Louis. Who was he?

Q2 Name the slugger who came to the Senators after Washington sent Goose Goslin to the Tigers in a 1930 trade.

Q3 The Tigers traded this hurler to Washington for aces Firpo Marberry and Carl Fischer in 1933. Who came to the District in the transaction?

Q4 In a bizarre trade in 1938, the Senators sent the AL's best-fielding first baseman to the White Sox for the league's worst-fielding player at that position. Name the men exchanged.

Q5 In 1950, two-time batting champ Mickey Vernon came to the District from Cleveland in return for a pitcher known as "Legs." Who was that ace?

Q6 Who was sent to Cleveland in an October 1961 trade that brought Jimmy Piersall to the Senators?

Q7 The Senators dispatched two players to the Dodgers in return for Ken McMullen, Dick Nen, Frank Howard, Phil Ortega, and Pete Richert. Who was dealt to La La Land in the 1964 blockbuster deal?

Q8 Gil Hodges was sent to the New York Mets in 1967 for $100,000 and what right-handed pitcher?

Q9 Only once in major league history in 1968, have two players been traded for one another twice in the same season. The clubs involved were the Senators and the White Sox. Name the players exchanged.

Q10 Curt Flood balked at his 1969 trade from St. Louis to the Phillies, and eventually signed with the Senators in 1971 after sitting out one season. What three players did Washington send to Philadelphia as compensation for signing Flood?

WASHINGTON SENATORS

A1   General Crowder

A2   Heinie Manush (and pitcher Alvin Crowder)

A3   Earl Whitehill

A4   Washington sent Joe Kuhel to Chicago for Zeke Bonura.

A5   Dick Weik

A6   Dick Donovan

A7   John Kennedy
Claude Osteen (and $100,000)

A8   Bill Denehy

A9   Ron Hansen and Tim Cullen

A10   Greg Goossen
Jerry Terpko
Gene Martin
(None of the three ever played a game in the majors after the trade.)

*** FAST FACTS ***

Opening day of the 1910 season was a memorable one as the Senators' Walter Johnson tossed a one-hitter en route to a 3–0 victory over the A's. In that same game, William Howard Taft became the first U.S. president to throw a ceremonial first pitch.

Calvin Griffith was actually Clark Griffith's nephew, the son of his deceased brother. Clark adopted Calvin when he was a youngster.

Hall of Famer "Big Ed" Delahanty made a big splash on and off the field. While playing ball, he led the majors in batting average twice, RBIs three times, and once for homers. His life ended in 1903 when he was ejected from a train for being drunk and disorderly, fell off a bridge, and was swept over Niagara Fallas.

Filipino Dave Altizer, who played with the Senators in the early 1900s, invented a postcard in 1908 with a photo of William Jennings Bryan that, when held up to the light, also depicted a picture of the White House.

Washington Bullets

WASHINGTON BULLETS

Washington Bullet Mascot Tiny

THE SUITS

Q1   Since 1970, these two former Bullet coaches rank No. 1 and No. 2 as the NBA's all-time leaders in technical fouls. Who are they?

Q2   Which former Bullet skipper has two NCAA championship trophies and an Olympic Gold Medal on his mantel?

Q3   Gene Shue had the longest tenure of any Bullet coach, with 11 full and two partial seasons. Who had the shortest reign?

Q4   Who was the first Bullet coach to open two consecutive seasons?

Q5   Who was the attorney and insurance executive who brought pro basketball back to Baltimore in 1963?

Q6   The club's first general manager was a former Purdue All-American, NBA Rookie of the Year, and Bullet player-coach. Name him.

Q7   Who was the Bullets' first coach?

Q8   The second coach of the Bullets was a fixture in Baltimore basketball twenty years earlier. Name the man selected to head the team in 1964.

Q9   In what year did Abe Pollin buy the Baltimore franchise?

Q10   What construction novelty did Abe Pollin introduce?

Q11   Prior to coaching Baltimore during the 1965–66 season, Paul Seymour was at the helm of two other teams. Name them.

Q12   Who drafted Mike Farmer with their number one pick (third pick overall) in the 1958 draft?

WASHINGTON BULLETS

A1   Dick Motta (357)
         Kevin Loughery (335)

A2   K. C. Jones

A3   Mike Farmer (1966–67: nine games, a 1–8 record)

A4   Gene Shue (1967–68 and 1968–69)

A5   Dave Trager (Trager bought the Chicago franchise and relocated it to Baltimore in 1963.)

A6   Paul Hoffman

A7   Bob Leonard (1963–64)

A8   Buddy Jeannette

A9   1964 (He, Arnold Heft, and Earl Foreman purchased the club for a then-record of $1.1 million)

A10   He was the first to build swimming pools on the rooftops of apartment buildings.

A11   Syracuse Nationals (1956–57 through 1959–60)
         St. Louis Hawks (1960–61 through 1961–62)

A12   New York Knicks

Q13 Mike Farmer played with two Hall of Famers on his collegiate team. Name them.

Q14 Bob Ferry was named *The Sporting News* Basketball Executive of the Year twice—1978–79 and 1981–82. Who are the only two men besides Ferry to be honored twice with this award?

Q15 Besides playing for the club, Bob Ferry assumed two other responsibilities with the Bullets during the 1968–69 season. What were they?

Q16 What club selected Bob Ferry with its number one collegiate draft pick (seventh pick overall) in 1959?

Q17 Gene Shue was a first-round selection (third pick overall) in the 1954 collegiate draft. What team chose the University of Maryland product?

Q18 What five clubs did Gene Shue play for during his NBA playing career?

Q19 How old was Gene Shue when he took over as coach of the Bullets in 1967?

Q20 Gene Shue is one of four men to have been named Coach of the Year twice. Who are the other three recipients?

Q21 For what club was K. C. Jones head coach during the 1972–73 season?

Q22 Bernie Bickerstaff turned down a pro basketball playing career so that he could accept the assistant coaching position at San Diego State. Who wanted Bickerstaff to play for them?

Q23 Under what three head coaches did Bernie Bickerstaff serve as assistant coach?

Q24 Bernie Bickerstaff left the Bullets in 1985 to assume the head coaching duties with what NBA team?

Q25 When Dick Motta was named coach of the Bullets in 1976–77, this player declared that he'd rather give up the game than play for such a man. Who made the claim?

Q26 What team attempted to lure Dick Motta to the ABA in the early 1970s?

Q27 Kevin Loughery originally came to the Bullets in 1963 from Detroit. What player was traded to the Pistons in the deal?

WASHINGTON BULLETS

A13 Bill Russell
K. C. Jones
(Farmer was a member of San Francisco University from 1954 through 1958.)

A14 Phoenix's GM Jerry Colangelo
Atlanta's Stan Kasten

A15 Assistant coach
Scout

A16 St. Louis Hawks

A17 Philadelphia Warriors

A18 Philadelphia Warriors (1954)
New York Knicks (1954–55, 1962–63)
Fort Wayne Pistons (1956–57)
Detroit Pistons (1957–58 through 1961–62)
Baltimore Bullets (1963–64)

A19 35 years old

A20 Bill Fitch (1975–76: Cleveland; 1979–80: Boston)
Don Nelson (1984–85: Milwaukee; 1991–92: Golden State)
Cotton Fitzsimmons (1978–79: Kansas City; 1988–89: Phoenix)

A21 ABA San Diego Conquistadors

A22 Harlem Globetrotters

A23 K. C. Jones
Dick Motta
Gene Shue

A24 Seattle SuperSonics

A25 Elvin Hayes (who did show up for training camp)

A26 Dallas Chaparrals

A27 Larry Staverman

THE SUITS

Q28 Kevin Loughery lost four teeth and was knocked out of action for several games when he was punched in the mouth during a 1963 Bullet game. Name the San Francisco Warrior who landed the right.

Q29 Kevin Loughery was put out of action for the balance of the 1969–70 season when a collision resulted in a punctured lung and cracked ribs. Whose knee caused the damage to the Bullet guard?

Q30 What four clubs did Kevin Loughery coach prior to coming to Washington on March 19, 1986?

Q31 How many games were left in the 1985–86 season when Kevin Loughery took over the Bullets' coaching reins from Gene Shue?

Q32 What was Kevin Loughery's nickname?

Q33 Wes Unseld played his last NBA game on March 29, 1981. What club did Washington defeat that evening at home?

Q34 Wes Unseld took over as coach of the Bullets just 22 games into the 1987–88 season. What was Washington's record at the time?

Q35 Wes Unseld reached his 10,000th career point on March 11, 1980. Who was Washington playing that evening?

Q36 The 1968 draft, in which Wes Unseld was selected by the Bullets, was the most unique in NBA history because four centers were picked with the top four choices. Who were these tall selections?

Q37 What two awards did Wes Unseld snare in 1968–69, his first year in the NBA?

THE UNIFORMS

Q1 What former first-round pick of the St. Louis Hawks did Wes Unseld succeed as the Bullets' pivot in 1968?

Q2 Who was the first Bullet to make an All-Star team?

Q3 Elvin Hayes appeared in the 1980 All-Star Game. Who was the next Bullet to be selected to the annual match?

WASHINGTON BULLETS

A28   Guy Rodgers

A29   Kareem Abdul-Jabbar's (then known as Lew Alcindor)

A30   Philadelphia 76ers (1972–73)
New York/New Jersey Nets (1973–74—1980–81)
Atlanta Hawks (1981–82—1982–83)
Chicago Bulls (1983–84—1984–85)

A31   13 (Loughery went 7–6 the rest of the way.)

A32   "Murph"

A33   Cleveland Cavaliers (138–103)

A34   8–19 (Unseld finished with a 30–25 record, for a 38–44 overall record.)

A35   San Antonio (The Spurs won 111–104 at the Capital Centre.)

A36   1—Elvin Hayes (San Diego Rockets)
2—Wes Unseld (Bullets)
3—Bob Kauffman (Seattle SuperSonics)
4—Tom Boerwinkle (Chicago Bulls)

A37   Rookie of the Year
Most Valuable Player

A1   Bob Ferry

A2   Gus Johnson (1964–65)

A3   Jeff Ruland (1984)

THE UNIFORMS

Q4   Who is the only Bullet to ever win the All-Star Game MVP Award?

Q5   Dick Motta coached the East in the 1979 All-Star Game. What two Bullets played in the contest?

Q6   Only one Bullet has ever led the league in personal fouls for a season. Who was it?

Q7   What Washington duo were nicknamed the "Beef Brothers"?

Q8   Who was the last member of the Chicago Packer franchise (1961–62) to play for the Bullets?

Q9   Who was the last player to remain with the Bullets from the club's inaugural (1963–64) season?

Q10   Gus Johnson finished second in the balloting for the 1963–64 Rookie of the Year honor. Who edged him out?

Q11   Gus Johnson played high school ball in Akron, Ohio, with what other NBA great?

Q12   With what club did Gus Johnson finish his professional basketball career?

Q13   Gus Johnson was tied in 1963–64 as the league leader in disqualifications. Who shared his mark of 11 ejections?

Q14   Sihugo Green was the first overall pick in the 1956 draft. Players chosen after him included Bill Russell, Tom Heinsohn, and K. C. Jones. What team selected Green?

Q15   Walt Bellamy finished second in field goal accuracy for the 1964–65 season. Who topped his .509 percentage by a mere .001?

Q16   What two Bullets led the club in personal fouls in the 1963–64 season?

Q17   The first Bullet to shatter a backboard did so during a November 24, 1964 away game against the St. Louis Hawks. Who slammed the boards that evening?

Q18   This Villanova guard was acquired by the Bullets in a 1964 trade before he played one pro game. He was Villanova's MVP in both his junior and senior years, and was selected MVP of New York's 1963 Holiday Festival. Name him.

Q19   What club originally drafted Don Ohl in the fifth round of the 1958 draft?

WASHINGTON BULLETS

A4   Dave Bing (1976)

A5   Elvin Hayes
Bob Dandridge

A6   Kevin Porter (1973–74: 319)

A7   Rick Mahorn
Jeff Ruland

A8   Walt Bellamy (1965–66)

A9   Gus Johnson (1963–64 through 1971–72)

A10   Cincinnati's Jerry Lucas

A11   Nate Thurmond

A12   Indiana Pacers of the ABA (1972–73)

A13   Zelmo Beaty (St. Louis Hawks)

A14   Rochester Royals

A15   Wilt Chamberlain

A16   Gus Johnson
Terry Dischinger
(Each had 321 personal fouls.)

A17   Gus Johnson

A18   Wali Jones

A19   Philadelphia Warriors (He was traded to Detroit before he ever played a game with them.)

Q20 Who broke Johnny Kerr's "iron man" record of 834 consecutive games?

Q21 Johnny Kerr played on three teams in setting this record. Name them.

Q22 Selected in the 1965 supplemental draft, this player was the nation's top scorer in 1964–65 with a 39.4 average at Miles Memorial College. He played in five Bullet games in the 1965–66 season, scored six points, and never played another pro game. Name him.

Q23 Drafted in the seventh round of the 1965 draft, this player was the greatest scorer up to that time at Duquesne. When he entered the NBA in 1965, he was the shortest player on any roster (5′10″). After only eight games with the Bullets, he went to the ABA, where he played two seasons. Who is he?

Q24 During his seven-year pro career, Jim Barnes played with five different teams. Who originally drafted the center in the first round in 1964?

Q25 Earl Monroe was the second overall selection in the 1967 draft. Who was chosen ahead of "the Pearl"?

Q26 What college did Earl Monroe attend?

Q27 A 1967 first-round pick of the St. Louis Hawks, this cager was acquired by Baltimore during the 1967–68 season. Four minutes into his first Bullet game, he turned his knee and was lost for the year. Name him.

Q28 What NBA great shared backcourt responsibilities with Archie Clark at the University of Minnesota?

Q29 In what round was Mike Riordan plucked by the Knicks in the 1967 draft?

Q30 Phil Chenier was the Bullets' first-round selection in the NBA's special "Hardship Draft" in 1971. At what college was Chenier a two-year starter?

Q31 In 1971, Bob Ferry spotted Phil Chenier on a scouting trip, but Chenier wasn't the original object of Ferry's travels. Who drew the Bullet scout to the University of California's basketball game?

Q32 This 1971 first-round draft pick played two seasons with the Bullets and four seasons overall in the NBA. His brother is famous as a member of a musical group. Name the player.

Q33 In the 1969–70 season, Elvin Hayes won the NBA rebounding title, making him the first person in 12 seasons to win the honor besides Wilt Chamberlain and Bill Russell. Who was the last person before Wilt and Russell to have won the honor?

WASHINGTON BULLETS

A20   Randy Smith (906 games)

A21   Syracuse Nationals (1954–55 through 1963–64)
Philadelphia 76ers (1964–65)
Baltimore Bullets (1965–66)

A22   Thales McReynolds

A23   Willie Somerset

A24   New York Knicks

A25   Jimmy Walker (by the Detroit Pistons)

A26   Winston-Salem

A27   Tom Workman

A28   Lou Hudson

A29   The 12th

A30   University of California

A31   Charles Johnson

A32   Stan Love (His brother Mike is a member of the Beach Boys.)

A33   Rochester Royal Maurice Stokes (1956–57)

Q34   Elvin Hayes scored his 20,000th NBA point on December 13, 1978. What club was Washington playing that evening?

Q35   In the time that Elvin Hayes played for the Bullets, he led the club in scoring seven times. Who was the only other player to lead the team in scoring between 1971–72 and 1981–82?

Q36   On February 12, 1978, Big E became the Bullets' all-time leading scorer. Who held the club record previous to Hayes?

Q37   In what year of his career was Elvin Hayes selected as a first-team All-Star?

Q38   The Bullets signed Kevin Porter as a free agent in 1979. What did the club give up to Detroit to reclaim the guard?

Q39   A second-round pick in the 1972 draft from Ouachita Baptist University, this Bullet served a year in Vietnam. Who was he?

Q40   When Tom Kozelko was picked in the third round of the 1973 draft, he was the No. 2 scorer in Toledo history. Who was Toledo's all-time leading scorer?

Q41   What club selected Clem Haskins with the third overall pick in the 1967 draft?

Q42   Jimmy Jones played seven seasons in the ABA before joining the Bullets in 1974. What three teams did he play with prior to coming to Washington?

Q43   Dave Bing was the second overall pick in the 1966 draft when he was taken by Detroit. Who was taken ahead of him?

Q44   When Dave Bing joined the Bullets in 1975, he was the third-leading scorer among active players in the NBA. Who were ahead of him?

Q45   At the time Dave Bing became a Bullet he was one of only four guards to lead the NBA in scoring for a season. Who were the other three?

Q46   On December 16, 1979, Kevin Grevey "bumped" a referee while arguing a call in a game with the Bulls at the Capital Centre. He was subsequently fined $1,000 and suspended for one game. Name the ref he "roughed up."

Q47   When Kevin Grevey graduated, he left Kentucky as the school's No. 2 all-time scorer. Who was first?

Q48   What football club drafted Tom Kropp in the eighth round of the 1975 NFL draft with hopes of signing the collegiate linebacker?

WASHINGTON BULLETS

A34   San Diego Clippers

A35   Phil Chenier (1973–74 and 1975–76)

A36   Kevin Loughery

A37   His seventh (1974–75)

A38   Its first-round picks in 1980 and 1982

A39   Tom Patterson

A40   Steve Mix

A41   Chicago Bulls

A42   New Orleans Buccaneers (1967–68 through 1969–70)
Memphis Pros (1970–71)
Utah Stars (1971–72 through 1973–74)

A43   Cazzie Russell (New York Knicks)

A44   Boston's John Havlicek
Chicago's Chet Walker

A45   Max Zaslofsky (1947–48: Chicago Stags)
Jerry West (1969–70: L.A. Lakers)
Nate Archibald (1972–73: K.C.-Omaha Kings)
(Bing won in 1967–68 while playing for the Pistons.)

A46   Hugh Evans

A47   Dan Issel

A48   Pittsburgh Steelers

Q49　This Bullet was the first overall selection in the 1976 draft (though it wasn't Washington that selected him). Name the player and the team that made him the top choice.

Q50　Charles Johnson played on two championship teams in his seven-year NBA career. One was the 1977–78 Bullets. What was the other?

Q51　On January 24, 1978, with the Bullets' guards decimated by injury, GM Bob Ferry telephoned a free agent, signed him, and flew him to Washington from the West Coast, all on the same day. That evening, he played in a Washington game and scored six points against the Pistons. Who is he?

Q52　A first-round pick (14th overall) of the Bullets in 1978, this guard was used sparingly for one and a half seasons before he was dealt to New Jersey. He would play for five different clubs over his six-year career. Name him.

Q53　This Washington free agent signee was the first player to be named the NBA's Comeback Player of the Year (1981). Name him.

Q54　When Don Collins graduated from Washington State in 1980, he ranked third on the all-time Pac-10 career scoring list. Who was ranked ahead of him?

Q55　Jim Chones began his pro career in the ABA in 1972. For what two ABA clubs did Chones play before coming to the NBA?

Q56　Washington acquired Jeff Ruland on June 10, 1980, but did not come to terms with the Iona center until May 21, 1981. Where did Ruland play in the interim?

Q57　What club drafted Jeff Ruland in the 1980 NBA draft?

Q58　Spencer Haywood was named the ABA's Rookie of the Year and MVP for the 1969–70 season. What club was he playing with?

Q59　In 1981–82, Spencer Haywood finished second in voting for the NBA's Comeback Player of the Year, the same season that the 33-year-old forward joined Washington. Who edged out Haywood for the honor?

Q60　Spencer Haywood joined the Bullets in 1981, but his biggest impact on the club and the NBA occurred in the legal courts in 1971. What did Haywood's lawsuit do to pro basketball?

Q61　Who set a collegiate record for assists in 1982–83 when he averaged 11.0 assists per game (319 for the season) while playing for California State-Fullerton?

WASHINGTON BULLETS

A49   John Lucas (Maryland)
Houston Rockets

A50   Golden State Warriors (1974–75)

A51   Charles Johnson (Washington won that evening, 104–101.)

A52   Roger Phegley

A53   Bernard King (while playing for Golden State)

A54   Ron Lee
Kareem Abdul-Jabbar

A55   New York Nets (1972–73)
Carolina Cougars (1973–74)

A56   Spain

A57   Golden State Warriors (Ruland was selected with the second overall pick in the second round.)

A58   Denver Nuggets

A59   Seattle's Gus Williams

A60   It forced the league to grant admission to underclassmen even though their college classes had not yet graduated.

A61   Leon Wood

Q62 Jeff Malone's 1986–87 free throw percentage, .885, was third best in Bullet history. What two Washington players have had better single-season averages?

Q63 When drafted in 1983, Jeff Malone was Mississippi State's all-time leading scorer, with 2,142 career points. What former Bullet held the school mark prior to Malone?

Q64 Jeff Malone averaged 24.3 points per game in the 1989–90 season. Who was the last Bullet guard to average as many points?

Q65 What team originally drafted Maryland's Tom McMillen with a 1974 first-round choice?

Q66 Tom McMillen delayed his arrival in the NBA for one year after being drafted. Why did he postpone his premiere in the NBA?

Q67 What club originally picked Cliff Robinson in the first round of the 1979 draft?

Q68 Between the time he was released by Phoenix in 1982 and the time he was signed by Washington on September 27, 1984, Dudley Bradley was signed by two different clubs as a free agent (but never played in a game for either). What clubs signed and then released the guard?

Q69 Gus Williams became the NBA's all-time leader in steals (since broken) when he recorded steal number 1,404 on December 15, 1984. Against what team did he break the record?

Q70 Who surpassed Gus Williams's all-time NBA steal record of 1,638?

Q71 Charles Jones had three brothers who played in the NBA. Name them.

Q72 Manute Bol established himself quickly as one of the league's premier defensive players. In the 1985–86 seasons, his first year, Bol was named to the NBA's All-Defensive Team and was runner-up in the Defensive Player of the Year voting. Who edged him out for the award?

Q73 In his first season, Manute Bol led the league by rejecting 397 shots, the second-best single-season mark in NBA history. Who set the mark by blocking 456 in one season?

Q74 Manute Bol has a daughter, Atong, and three sons—Abuk, Madut, and Chris. Who did he name his last son after?

Q75 At 7'7", Manute Bol is the tallest player in the history of the NBA. Who was the tallest before Bol appeared on the court?

WASHINGTON BULLETS

A62 Jack Marin (1971–72: .894)
Larry Wright (1979–80: .889)

A63 Bailey Howell

A64 Archie Clark (1971–72: 25.1)

A65 Buffalo Braves

A66 He accepted a Rhodes scholarship to England's Oxford University after graduating from Maryland.

A67 New Jersey Nets

A68 Chicago Bulls
Detroit Pistons

A69 L.A. Clippers

A70 Maurice Cheeks (1,942)

A71 Caldwell Jones
Will Jones
Major Jones

A72 San Antonio's Alvin Robertson

A73 Utah's Mark Eaton (1984–85)

A74 Golden State's Chris Mullin (Bol's former teammate)

A75 Utah's Mark Eaton (7'4")

Q17. Gene Shue was a first-round selection (third pick overall) in the 1954 collegiate draft. What team chose the University of Maryland product?

WASHINGTON BULLETS

Q31. In 1971, Bob Ferry spotted Phil Chenier on a scouting trip, but Chenier wasn't the original object of Ferry's travels. Who drew the Bullet scout to the University of California's basketball game?

Q36. On February 12, 1978, Big E became the Bullets all-time leading scorer. Who held the club record previous to Hayes?

WASHINGTON BULLETS

Q45. At the time Dave Bing became a Bullet, he was one of only four guards to ever lead the NBA in scoring for a season. Who were the other three?

THE UNIFORMS

Q76   Manute Bol was drafted in 1985 by Washington after the center finished one year of college. What school did Bol attend?

Q77   Manute Bol twice recorded 15 blocked shots in a game—versus Atlanta in 1986 and against Indiana in 1987. Who is the only NBA player to have more blocked shots in one game?

Q78   Anthony Jones was drafted in 1986 out of UNLV, where he played his junior and senior years. Where did Jones play his first two years of collegiate ball?

Q79   Darwin Cook left Portland University in 1980 as the school's all-time leader in points, assists, and steals. Who later surpassed his scoring title there?

Q80   Jay Vincent was a unanimous All-Rookie choice in 1981−82 when he averaged 21.4 points per game, fifteenth best in the NBA that season. What two players finished ahead of Vincent for Rookie of the Year honors that season?

Q81   John Williams was suspended for the entire 1991−92 season by Wes Unseld. Why?

Q82   John Williams was the third LSU Tiger to score over 600 points in a season. Who were the first two?

Q83   In what year, and with what team, did Bernard King win the NBA scoring title?

Q84   Bernard King ranked third in the league for scoring in the 1990−91 season (28.4 average). When was the last time that a Bullet finished as high as third among the annual scoring leaders?

Q85   When Mark Alarie graduated from Duke in 1986, he was the school's fourth all-time leading scorer. Who was ahead of him?

Q86   Moses Malone was one of three players to enter the pro ranks directly from high school. Who were the other two?

Q87   Prior to coming to the Bullets, Moses Malone played for three NBA clubs. Name them.

Q88   Tyrone Bogues played basketball at Dunbar High School on a team that fielded two other future NBA players. Name Bogues's teammates.

WASHINGTON BULLETS

A76   University of Bridgeport

A77   Laker Elmore Smith (1973: 17 blocked shots)

A78   Georgetown

A79   Indiana Pacer Jose Slaughter

A80   New Jersey's Buck Williams (winner)
           Detroit's Kelly Tripucka (runner-up)

A81   He was overweight and failed his physical.

A82   Bob Pettit
           Pete Maravich

A83   1984–85: New York Knicks (32.9-point average)

A84   Earl Monroe (1968–69: Monroe finished second with a 24.3-point average
           behind Houston's Elvin Hayes, who averaged 25.4).

A85   Johnny Dawkins
           Mike Gminski
           Danny Ferry

A86   Bill Willoughby
           Darryl Dawkins

A87   Buffalo Braves (1976–77)
           Houston Rockets (1976–77 through 1981–82)
           Philadelphia 76ers (1982–83 through 1985–86)

A88   Reggie Williams
           Reggie Lewis

Q89 Dave Feitl finished his collegiate career at the University of Texas at El Paso as the second-highest career scorer at that school. Who was first?

Q90 Greg Foster was drafted by the Bullets in 1990 from UTEP in the second round, but Foster did not start his collegiate career at that school. What college did he leave in the midst of the 1987–88 season?

Q91 Bullet Larry Robinson has a cousin who also played in the NBA. Who is Robinson's relative?

Q92 During the 1990–91 season, Larry Robinson had two tenures with the Bullets. In between jobs with Washington, he played 24 games with another NBA club. With who else did Robinson play that year?

Q93 What league award did Pervis Ellison snag in 1992?

Q94 Three members of Louisville's starting five from the 1986 NCAA championship team made it to the pros. Pervis Ellison was one of the those Cardinals. Who are the other two?

Q95 Pervis Ellison scored 2,143 career points in college, making him only the second Louisville player to reach the 2,000-point plateau. Who is the other Cardinal to reach that level?

Q96 The Bullets drafted LaBradford Smith with the 19th overall pick in the 1991 NBA draft. What baseball club drafted Smith out of high school in 1986?

Q97 During his first season with the Bullets, Michael Adams made the All-Star Team for the first time in his career. What superstar did he replace in the annual classic?

Q98 Michael Adams set an NBA record during the 1991–92 season for career four-point plays (a three-point basket plus a foul shot). How many does he have (as of November 1992)?

Q99 Michael Adams set an NBA record for consecutive games in which he hit at least one three-point field goal. For how many games does his record extend?

Q100 Michael Adams broke the Bullets' franchise records for three-point field goals attempted (386) and made (125) in a season. Who held those club marks before Adams?

Q101 The Bullets received Michael Adams and the 19th overall selection in the 1991 draft from Denver in exchange for the eighth overall pick in the 1991 draft. Who did the Nuggets choose with the selection?

WASHINGTON BULLETS

A89 Nate "Tiny" Archibald (1,459 points)
(Feitl finished with 1,422 points)

A90 UCLA (He left the California school 11 games into the season.)

A91 Celtic Robert Parrish

A92 Golden State Warriors

A93 Most Improved Player

A94 Billy Thompson
Milt Wagner

A95 Darrell Griffith (2,333 points)

A96 Kansas City Royals

A97 Larry Bird

A98 Eight

A99 79 (spanning the 1987–88 and 1988–89 seasons)

A100 Kevin Grevey

A101 Temple's Mark Macon

Q102   Buck Johnson developed his patented "jump-hook" at Alabama to counter two conference rivals. What two collegiate seven-footers influenced Johnson's shooting style?

Q103   Buck Johnson is the fourth-leading scorer in Alabama history, with 1,896 points. Who ranks ahead of him in Crimson Tide annals?

Q104   Rex Chapman was just the third player in Kentucky's history to surpass 1,000 career points in only his second year at the school. What other Wildcats had achieved that point total by the end of their sophomore season?

FYI

Q1   First they were the Baltimore Bullets, then they became the Capital Bullets. In what year did the franchise finally change the name to the Washington Bullets?

Q2   What franchise was moved to Baltimore and renamed the Bullets on June 4, 1963?

Q3   What other franchise changed cities the same year that the Bullets were born?

Q4   The year the Bullets came into existence, 1963, was the same year that the NBA experienced a changing of the guard. Who were the outgoing and incoming league presidents that season?

Q5   Who did the first play-by-play announcing for the Bullets?

Q6   The Bullets were shifted from the Western to the Eastern Division in 1966–67 to accommodate what expansion club?

Q7   In what year did the Bullets move down the I-490 from Baltimore to Landover?

Q8   What team did the Bullets tip off against on opening night at the Capital Centre?

Q9   Who scored the first basket ever made at the Capital Centre?

WASHINGTON BULLETS

A102   Sam Bowie
Mel Turpin
(both from Kentucky)

A103   Reggie King
Eddie Phillips
Leon Douglas

A104   Cotton Nash
Dan Issel

A1   1974 (April 20)

A2   Chicago Zephyrs

A3   The Nationals left Syracuse to become the Philadelphia 76ers.

A4   Maurice Podoloff (the NBA's first and, until then only president) left. J. Walter Kennedy assumed the position.

A5   Jim Karvellas

A6   Chicago Bulls

A7   1973 (April)

A8   Seattle SuperSonics (The Bullets won, 98–96.)

A9   Bud Stallworth (of the SuperSonics)

Q10 The Bullets have played four games overseas in their existence. Name the cities that have hosted the D.C. hoopsters.

Q11 The Bullets hosted the 1980 All-Star Game, the first ever held in D.C. Name the East and West coaches from that year.

Q12 Who was the MVP of that Capital Centre contest?

SETTING THE STANDARD

Q1 Who was the first NBA player to surpass the 1,000-assist mark in a season?

Q2 The Bullets hold the NBA record for fewest assists in a game. What is that low mark?

Q3 Who were the Bullets facing on October 16, 1963, when the team set the NBA record for fewest assists in a game?

Q4 Elvin Hayes is the Bullets' all-time leader in blocked shots, with 1,558. Who ranks second on the club's list?

Q5 What Bullet bettered the NBA record for field goal accuracy in 1965–66 with a .536 mark?

Q6 Who is the Bullets' best career field goal percentage performer?

Q7 Who holds the Bullets' single-season record for highest field goal percentage?

Q8 What opposing player set dual Bullet records when he attempted 39 field goals and made 23 of them in one game?

Q9 Jack Marin holds the club record for the highest single-season free throw percentage (1971–72: .894). Who holds the club record for free throws made in one year?

Q10 Who is the Bullets' all-time free throw percentage leader in the playoffs (minimum: 40 made)?

Q11 During the 1974–75 season, the Bullets equaled a league record for home court victories. Of the 41 games played at home, how many victories did they have?

WASHINGTON BULLETS

A10   Tel Aviv, Israel (1978)
Beijing, China (1979)
Shanghai, China (1979)
Manilla, Philippines (1979)

A11   East: Billy Cunningham
West: Lenny Wilkens
(The East won, 144–136, in overtime.)

A12   San Antonio's George Gervin

A1   Kevin Porter (1978–79: 1,099 assists as a Piston)

A2   Three

A3   Boston Celtics

A4   Charlie Jones (910)

A5   Johnny Green (He was 358 for 668. That same season, Wilt Chamberlain
established a new NBA record with a .540 mark.)

A6   Jeff Ruland (.564)

A7   Jeff Ruland (1983–84: 599 for 1,035; .579)

A8   Pete Maravich (December 26, 1976: at New Orleans)

A9   Earl Monroe (1969–70: 532)

A10   Frank Johnson (46 of 50: .920)

A11   36

Q12 Name the former Bullet who once established a record (since broken) for most consecutive games played.

Q13 Name the Bullet who set two club single-season marks by playing 3,602 minutes and averaging 44.5 minutes per game.

Q14 The Bullets hold the NBA record for most consecutive seasons with 35 or more victories. What is the team's streak?

Q15 Only two Bullets have ever scored more than 2,000 points in a season. Name them.

Q16 Who holds the Bullets' mark for scoring in a playoff game?

Q17 What opponent once scored 56 points against the Bullets—the most they've ever given up to one player?

Q18 Identify the sharpshooter who set a franchise record for three-pointers made (125) and attempted (386) in one season, 1991–92.

Q19 This opponent cleared the boards when he pulled down 33 rebounds in a contest against the Bullets. Who holds this team record?

Q20 Who set an NBA rookie record by netting a .572 field goal percentage?

Q21 Who has the highest career playoff scoring average in Bullet history? (minimum: 200 points)

Q22 Phil Chenier set Washington's single-season record by averaging 2.29 steals per game in 1974–75. Who holds the club mark with 178 steals in one year?

Q23 What two Bullets have registered nine steals in one game?

Q24 Who holds the Bullet career record for turnovers?

GLORY DAYS

Q1 This Bullet grabbed 34 rebounds in a 1970 playoff game against the Knicks—more than the entire New York team. Who was the Bullets' chairman of the boards?

Q2 Why was the showdown between the Bullets and Warriors in the 1974–75 finals a historic moment in sports history?

WASHINGTON BULLETS

A12   Johnny Kerr (October 31, 1954—November 4, 1965: 844 games)

A13   Elvin Hayes (1973–74)

A14   22 (1967–68 through 1988–89)

A15   Walt Bellamy (1961–62: 2,495 points
1962–63: 2,233
1963–64: 2,159
Earl Monroe (1968–69: 2,065)

A16   Elvin Hayes (April 25, 1975: 46 points vs. Buffalo)

A17   Wilt Chamberlain (December 1, 1964: at San Francisco)

A18   Michael Adams

A19   Kevin Willis (February 19, 1992: at Atlanta)

A20   Mitch Kupchak (1976–77: 341 for 596)

A21   Don Ohl (13 games: 341 points; 26.2 points per game)

A22   Gus Williams (1984–85)

A23   Gus Williams (10-30-84: vs. Altanta)
Michael Adams (11-1-91: vs. Indiana)

A24   Jeff Ruland (1,176)

---   ·   ---

A1   Wes Unseld

A2   It marked the first time in a major American sports championship that both opposing coaches were black (K. C. Jones and Al Attles).

Q3   Rick Barry said the Warriors' 1975 victory over the Bullets was the greatest upset in the history of the NBA Finals. What was the series' record?

Q4   The Bullets met the Hawks in the first round of the 1978 playoffs. Whose career-high 41 points led Washington to victory in the second game and allowed the Bullets to sweep Atlanta, 2–0?

Q5   In the first game of the 1978 Eastern Conference Finals, Washington defeated the 76ers in overtime, 122–117.. Who scored the last seven points of the game for the Bullets?

Q6   In the sixth game of the 1978 Eastern Conference Finals, the Bullets and 76ers were tied at 99 with 12 seconds left in the game. Whose tip-in gave Washington a 101–99 victory and the series?

Q7   In the initial game of the 1978 NBA Finals, the Bullets dominated the SuperSonics for three quarters, but Seattle outscored Washington 33–18 in the fourth period to win the contest. Whose 16 fourth-quarter points led the Sonics' comeback?

Q8   Washington set a Championship Series record in Game 6 of the 1978 finals by defeating Seattle by the largest margin in NBA history. What was the point difference?

Q9   Who sank a 55-foot shot at the third-quarter buzzer during the seventh game of the 1978 NBA Finals?

Q10   Who was the last member of the 1977–78 champion Bullets to play with the club?

Q11   What motto did Dick Motta live by during the finals of the 1977–78 showdown with Seattle?

Q12   What Sonic guard had an uncharacteristically cold shooting streak in Game 7 when he inexplicably missed each of the 14 shots he attempted?

Q13   When the Bullets whipped the Sonics for the 1977–78 NBA crown, it marked the first time the District had seen a championship in 36 years. What team brought glory to the nation's capital way back in 1942?

Q14   Who was Seattle's leading scorer when it defeated Washington for the 1978–79 world championship?

Q15   What two Sonic players accounted for more than half of Seattle's points in that series?

Q16   Who was the series MVP in that five-game contest?

WASHINGTON BULLETS

A3   Golden State swept the heavily favored Bullets, 4–0.

A4   Kevin Grevey

A5   Elvin Hayes

A6   Wes Unseld (He followed up his own shot to win the game.)

A7   "Downtown" Fred Brown

A8   35 points (117–82)

A9   Washington's Charles Johnson

A10   Greg Ballard (1984–85)

A11   "The Opera Isn't Over 'til the Fat Lady Sings"

A12   Dennis Johnson

A13   The NFL champion Redskins

A14   Gus Williams (25.9 ppg)

A15   Dennis Johnson
Gus Williams

A16   Dennis Johnson

TRADES, WAIVES, AND ACQUISITIONS

Q1 The first trade conducted by the Bullet franchise took place on September 6, 1963. Who did Baltimore sell to the Lakers?

Q2 Who was the Bullets' first-ever collegiate draft pick?

Q3 Who was the Bullets' number one draft pick in 1964?

Q4 A passel of players—Jim Barnes, Johnny Green, and Johnny Egan—came to the Bullets in exchange for one man in November 1965. Who went to the Knicks in the transaction?

Q5 Who did the Bullets send to L.A. for Leroy Ellis in 1966?

Q6 Bailey Howell was shipped to Boston in 1966 in exchange for what former Celtic?

Q7 In a three-way deal in 1967, Ray Scott came to the Bullets from Detroit. What other two players were involved in the transaction?

Q8 After drafting Earl Monroe with the club's first pick, the Bullets used the first pick of the second round in the 1967 draft to select this Grambling product. It would be seven years before he would play for them. Name him.

Q9 It was a flip of the coin that determined the first two slots in the 1968 draft, and Baltimore lost. Who won the toss, and who did that team select with the first overall choice?

Q10 What two players came to the Bullets in 1971 when Earl Monroe was traded to the Knicks on November 11, 1971?

Q11 Who did the Bullets send packing when the team acquired Elvin Hayes in a 1972 trade with Houston?

Q12 Who came to the Bullets when they sent two number three draft choices to Phoenix in October 1973?

Q13 The Bullets sent Stan Love to L.A. in exchange for cash and what former Laker?

Q14 On July 31, 1975, the Bullets acquired the Braves' first-round draft choice (13th overall pick in 1976) when they gave what player to Buffalo?

Q15 Name the backcourter who came to the Bullets in exchange for Dave Stallworth in a 1974 deal with Phoenix.

WASHINGTON BULLETS

A1   Don Nelson

A2   Rod Thorn (1963: West Virginia)

A3   Ohio State's Gary Bradds (Bradds played two seasons with the Bullets before leaving to play in the ABA.)

A4   Walt Bellamy

A5   Jim "Bad News" Barnes

A6   Mel Counts

A7   Mel Counts went from Baltimore to L.A.
Rudy LaRusso was sent to Detroit from L.A.

A8   Jimmy Jones

A9   San Diego Rockets
Elvin Hayes

A10   Mike Riordan
Dave Stallworth

A11   Jack Marin

A12   Walt Wesley

A13   Leonard "Truck" Robinson

A14   Dick Gibbs

A15   Clem Haskins

TRADES, WAIVES, AND ACQUISITIONS

Q16   The only player picked in the first round of both the NBA and ABA drafts in 1975 who was signed by an NBA team came to terms with the Bullets. Who is he?

Q17   Who did Washington send to Detroit when the Bullets acquired Dave Bing on August 28, 1975?

Q18   Nick Weatherspoon was traded to Seattle on December 14, 1976. Who came east in the deal?

Q19   Washington had two first-round choices in the 1976 draft. Who did the club select with the picks?

Q20   The Bullets had two 1977 first-round picks—the 14th and 17th picks overall. The second of the choices never played in Washington; he was traded to Denver before the start of the 1977–78 season. Name him.

Q21   Who did Washington send to Atlanta in 1977 in the deal that brought Tom Henderson to the Bullets?

Q22   The Bullets traded their first-round pick in 1979 to Phoenix. Who was the San Diego State forward-center who came to Washington in the deal?

Q23   Who did Washington give up in 1980 when the club received the San Antonio Spurs' second-round choices in the 1981 and 1982 draft?

Q24   For not matching the Lakers' offer to Mitch Kupchak, L.A. sent the Bullets two players. Name the duo.

Q25   Who did the Bullets dispatch to Atlanta when Don Collins was acquired from the Hawks on January 17, 1981?

Q26   The Bullets did not have a first-round pick in the 1982 draft, but did have three second-round choices. Who were the draftees?

Q27   Washington had the 10th and 22nd overall picks in the 1983 draft. Who were the club's choices?

Q28   Tim McCormick and Cliff Robinson were acquired from Cleveland on June 19, 1984. Who did the Bullets send to the Cavs in exchange?

Q29   Name the player who was selected in the first round (22nd overall) of the 1984 draft by the 76ers and was then traded to Washington for the Bullets' 1988 first-round pick.

Q30   Gus Williams came to the Bullets from Seattle on June 19, 1984. Who did Washington give up in the trade?

WASHINGTON BULLETS

A16 Kevin Grevey

A17 Kevin Porter

A18 Leonard Gray

A19 Mitch Kupchak (13th pick overall)
Larry Wright (14th pick overall)

A20 Marquette's Maurice "Bo" Ellis

A21 Leonard "Truck" Robinson

A22 Steve Malovic

A23 Dave Corzine

A24 Jim Chones
Brad Holland

A25 Wes Matthews

A26 Bryan Warrick (St. Joseph's)
Dwight Anderson (USC)
Mike Gibson (S.C. Spartanburg)

A27 Number 10: Jeff Malone
Number 22: Randy Wittman

A28 Melvin Turpin

A29 Tom Sewell

A30 Ricky Sobers
Tim McCormick

TRADES, WAIVES, AND ACQUISITIONS

Q31   Rick Mahorn and the rights to Mike Gibson were traded to Detroit on June 18, 1985. Who came to Washington in return?

Q32   The New Jersey Nets gave Darwin Cook to the Bullets so that Washington would not exercise its option of drafting what player?

Q33   The Bullets acquired the 21st overall pick in the 1986 draft from the 76ers as well as having their own choice (12th overall). Who did Washington draft with the selections?

Q34   The Bullets acquired Moses Malone, Terry Catledge, and the 76ers' 1986 and 1988 first-round draft picks in a 1986 trade. For what two players did Philly pay dearly?

Q35   The Bullets traded Jay Vincent and Michael Adams in a two-for-two deal with Denver on November 2, 1987. Who came to Washington in the transaction?

Q36   Who did Washington give up to obtain Sacramento King Pervis Ellison?

Q37   Who did Washington send to Charlotte on February 19, 1992, so that the Bullets could obtain Rex Chapman?

Q38   Name the pair of players who came east when the Bullets traded John Williams to the Clippers in an October 1992 deal.

WASHINGTON BULLETS

A31   Dan Roundfield

A32   Dwayne Washington

A33   12th: John Williams (LSU)
        21st: Anthony Jones (UNLV)

A34   Jeff Ruland
        Cliff Robinson

A35   Mark Alarie
        Darrell Walker

A36   Jeff Malone (plus a 1991 second-round draft pick)

A37   Tom Hammonds

A38   Don MacLean
        William Bedford

*** FAST FACTS ***

Abe Pollin is the longest-tenured owner in the NBA. (He bought the club in 1964.)

Bob Ferrick of the old Washington Caps did something in 1947–48 that no other player has accomplished: He led the league in field goal percentage (34.0) and free throw percentage (78.8) in the same season.

When playing the SuperSonics in Seattle, the Bullets stay at the Holiday Inn Crowne Plaza. The management installed a special 8-foot-long oversized bed for center Manute Bol.

With a 105–99 win over Seattle in the 1977–78 finals, the Bullets became only the third team in league annals to win the championship in a seventh game on the road.

Washington Capitals

THE SUITS

Q1   Which Cap majordomo was named Executive of the Year by *The Sporting News* in 1982–83?

Q2   In what industry did Abe Pollin make a name for himself by winning numerous awards and honors?

Q3   Where did Abe Pollin send his staff for training before the 1973 opening of the Capital Centre?

Q4   Who was the first coach to lead the Caps to a winning season?

Q5   Who was the Caps' first full-time assistant coach?

Q6   Known as the "Goaltending Guru," this skipper has the distinction of being the first Cap goaltending coach. Name him.

Q7   In the Caps' forgettable first season, 1974–75, three men coached the club. Identify the trio of skippers.

Q8   On what Stanley Cup team did Max McNab play in the early 1950s?

Q9   In what Paul Newman movie did former Cap coach Dan Belisle have a bit part?

Q10   When Gary Green was named head coach of the Capitals in November 1979, he became the youngest skipper in league history. How old was Green when he was named to the post?

Q11   Who took over the coaching reins for a single game after Gary Green was axed and before Bryan Murray took over behind the Washington bench on November 11, 1981?

WASHINGTON CAPITALS

A1   David Poile

A2   Construction

A3   Disney World

A4   Bryan Murray (1982–83: 39–25–16)

A5   Bill Mahoney (1980–81)

A6   Warren Strelow

A7   Jimmy Anderson (4–45–5)
George "Red" Sullivan (2–17–0)
Milt Schmidt (2–5)

A8   Detroit Red Wings

A9   *Slap Shot*

A10   27 years old

A11   Roger Crozier

THE SUITS

Q12   Bryan Murray worked at his alma mater as athletic director and hockey coach for four years. From what Montreal-based college did Murray graduate?

Q13   After compiling a 48–27–5 record in 1983–84 and sweeping the Flyers in the Patrick Division semis, Bryan Murray earned Coach of the Year honors. What is the name of the trophy Murray captured?

Q14   With what team did David Poile begin his career in hockey management?

Q15   Terry Murray was selected 88th overall in the 1970 Amateur Draft. What club chose Murray?

Q16   In his 12 years as a pro, Terry Murray played for Washington and three other NHL clubs. Name the teams.

Q17   Terry Murray was the first ex-player to coach the Caps. How long did he play for the franchise?

THE UNIFORMS

Q1   The Toronto Blizzard of the North American Soccer League at one time had this Cap on its roster. Name the versatile athlete.

Q2   Which former Cap rear guard lived for three years in Tehran, Iran, when he was a toddler?

Q3   Name the six players who have served as team captain.

Q4   Dubbed "The Man With the Golden Glove," this Washington goalie did not turn pro until he was 25 years old. Name the netminder.

Q5   What Washington player was nicknamed "Newsy"?

Q6   What Cap made his silver screen debut when he appeared with Rob Lowe in *Young Blood*?

Q7   Which Capital forward was born in Luck, USSR?

WASHINGTON CAPITALS

A12   McGill University

A13   Jack Adams Trophy

A14   Atlanta Flames (as an assistant general manager)

A15   California Golden Seals

A16   California Golden Seals
Detroit Red Wings
Philadelphia Flyers

A17   One season (1981–82)

A1   Peter Zezel

A2   Jim McTaggart

A3   Doug Mohns (1974–75)
Bill Clement (1975–76)
Yvon Labre (1976–77—1977–78)
Guy Charron (1978–79)
Ryan Walter (1979–80—1981–82)
Rod Langway (1982–83—present)

A4   Gary Inness

A5   Ron Lalonde

A6   Peter Zezel

A7   Peter Bondra

THE UNIFORMS

Q8   What trio made up the "Plumbers Line"?

Q9   This onetime Washington netminder was the NHL Rookie of the Year in 1965 and the winner of the Conn Smythe Trophy a year later. Identify this talented goalkeeper.

Q10   The nephew of football legend Bronko Nagurski, this Cap defenseman earned a bachelor's degree in economics from Harvard. Who was this Ivy Leaguer?

Q11   Which onetime Cap was the commissioner of an indoor ball-hockey league in Glens Falls, N.Y.?

Q12   Name the former Capital whose grandfather was Hockey Hall of Famer Dit Clapper.

Q13   Identify the pair of Capitals who played two seasons together at the University of New Hampshire in the mid-1970s.

Q14   Which Cap player was born in Taiwan?

Q15   What Washington forward was lauded as Clarkson College's Athlete of the Year in his senior year, 1979–80?

Q16   Who was the first Cap to wear Number 13?

Q17   Who was the only non-goalie Cap player to don Number 31?

Q18   Which former Cap teammates are distant cousins?

Q19   This man in the middle was the captain of the 1984 Canadian Olympic Team, a star player at the University of North Dakota, and the two-time winner of the Hartford Whalers' True Grit Award. Who is he?

Q20   Who led the team in scoring with 58 points during the team's inaugural season?

Q21   Ron Low has the distinction of being the first Cap goalie to record a shutout. Against what now-defunct team did Low get his big zero on February 16, 1975?

Q22   Who was the last skater from the original expansion team to play for the Caps?

WASHINGTON CAPITALS

A8   Greg Adams
Alan Haworth
Craig Laughlin

A9   Roger Crozier

A10   Neil Sheehy

A11   Al Jensen

A12   Greg Theberge

A13   Bob Gould
Rod Langway

A14   Rod Langway

A15   Craig Laughlin

A16   No player has worn that number.

A17   Archie Henderson

A18   Al Iafrate and Dino Ciccarelli

A19   Dave Tippett

A20   Tommy Williams (22–36: 58)

A21   Kansas City Scouts

A22   Yvon Labre (1974–81)

Q23   In 1980 Roger Crozier was inducted into the Buffalo Sabres Hall of Fame. Shortly after that honor, Crozier was voted one of the "23 Greatest Players" of all time by this NHL franchise. Which team so honored the former goalie?

Q24   How long did Roger Crozier suit up for the Caps when he was lured out of retirement by Max McNab during the 1976–77 season?

Q25   The 1976–77 roster included three players who would later become NHL general managers. Who are they?

Q26   The 1978–79 edition of the Washington Capitals had two black players on the team's roster. Name the tandem.

Q27   Bengt Gustafsson was a fourth-round pick of the Caps in the 1978 draft. He was also selected by a WHA team, where he saw action in one playoff game before his rights were transferred to Washington. With what WHA club did Gustafsson skate?

Q28   What NHL team did veteran centerman Dennis Hextall lead in scoring for three straight years (1973–75) and serve as the team's captain?

Q29   From what team was Dennis Maruk obtained in return for a first-round pick in the 1979 draft?

Q30   Among the freshman class of 1978–79 was Ryan Walter, who finished second overall in Calder Cup voting. Who edged out the Cap center for top rookie honors?

Q31   What was distinctive about Ryan Walter being named captain of the club in 1979–80?

Q32   It must have been déjà vu for Bengt Gustafsson when the centerman returned to the Caps after spending the 1986–87 season with another hockey club. For what team did Gustafsson play?

Q33   At age 19, Mike Gartner signed his first professional hockey contract with a WHA team. With what club did he suit up?

Q34   Name the trio who made up the "Roaring 20s" line.

Q35   Jean Pronovost spent most of his brilliant career in a Penguin uniform (1968–69—1977–78). He was traded to the Caps in the summer of 1980. With what now-defunct franchise did he play between stops in Pittsburgh and Washington?

WASHINGTON CAPITALS

A23 Detroit Red Wings

A24 Three games (Crozier was 1–0–0, playing a total of 103 minutes and earning a 1.17 goals-against average.)

A25 Roger Crozier
Gerry Meehan
Craig Patrick

A26 Mike Marson
Bill Riley

A27 Edmonton Oilers

A28 Minnesota North Stars

A29 Minnesota North Stars

A30 Bobby Smith (Minnesota North Stars)

A31 At 21, he was the youngest captain in league history.

A32 Bofors in Sweden

A33 Cincinnati Stingers (1978–79)

A34 Bob Kelly
Dennis Maruk
Jean Pronovost

A35 Atlanta Flames (1978–79—1979–80)

Q36   This well-traveled veteran signed with Washington as a free agent in 1981. A decade before, his first pro hockey coach was Max McNab at San Diego of the Western League. Who was this player?

Q37   In order to obtain Bobby Carpenter's rights, the Caps transferred their first- and second-round draft positions in exchange for this team's first- and third-round picks. With what club did the Caps play the trading game?

Q38   Which two players were chosen ahead of Bobby Carpenter in the 1981 draft?

Q39   When the Capitals drafted Bobby Carpenter in the top round of the 1981 draft, he was the first player to jump directly into the NHL from high school. From what school did Carpenter hail?

Q40   It took Bobby Carpenter a total of 23 minutes and six seconds to nail his first career NHL goal (October 7, 1981). Against what team did Carpenter light the lamp for his first-ever goal?

Q41   Bobby Carpenter shares a franchise record for most points in a game by a rookie (four). With what freshman player, who matched the work two days after Carpenter established it, does Carpenter co-own the honor?

Q42   What was noteworthy about Bob Carpenter's first 50-goal season (53 goals in 1984–85)?

Q43   Carpenter's 50 goals broke the previous record held by an American who played for the Blues. Who was that St. Louis skater?

Q44   What moniker was given to Bob Carpenter and Mike Gartner in 1984–85, the season the dynamic duo collected 50 or more goals each?

Q45   Name the Capital who led the league in penalty minutes during the 1982–83 season.

Q46   Doug Jarvis started his career in a Montreal uniform in 1975–76, but he had been drafted by another NHL team before the start of the season. Which franchise was it?

Q47   Doug Jarvis outpolled the Islanders' Bryan Trottier by seven votes to win the Selke Trophy after the 1983–84 campaign. What does the award signify?

Q48   Doug Jarvis played in 962 consecutive games from October 8, 1975 through April 5, 1987. Whose NHL record did Jarvis surpass on the way to setting the mark?

WASHINGTON CAPITALS

A36   Orest Kindrachuk

A37   Colorado Rockies

A38   Dale Hawerchuk (Winnipeg)
Doug Smith (Los Angeles)

A39   St. John's Prep (in Massachusetts)

A40   Buffalo Sabres (and goalie Don Edwards)

A41   Chris Valentine (Carpenter—vs. St. Louis; February 25, 1982
Valentine—vs. Hartford; February 27, 1982)

A42   Carpenter was the first American-born player to notch over 50 goals in a single season.

A43   Joe Mullen (41 goals)

A44   "The Goal Dust Twins"

A45   Randy Holt (275 minutes)

A46   Toronto Maple Leafs (The team traded his rights to Montreal.)

A47   The Selke Trophy is awarded to the league's top defensive forward.

A48   Garry Unger's (914 games)

Q22. Who was the last skater from the original expansion team to play for the Caps?

Q31. What was distinctive about Ryan Walter being named captain of the Caps in 1979–80?

Q7. He was the first player to reach the 100-point plateau in a Washington uniform. Name him.

Q49 Doug Jarvis's NHL record for consecutive games was accomplished over 12 seasons and while playing with three teams. Besides Washington, what clubs did Jarvis play for while setting the mark?

Q50 With what other NHL teams did Pat Riggin play before he was traded to Washington in 1982?

Q51 Although Rod Langway was originally drafted by the Canadiens, he played his first season of pro hockey for a WHA team. For what club did the All-Star defenseman play?

Q52 Who sported Number 5 before Rod Langway took over the digit in 1982?

Q53 When Rod Langway won the Norris Trophy (outstanding defenseman) in 1982–83, he became the first Cap to capture a major league award. What else was noteworthy about Langway's honor?

Q54 Scott Stevens's 1987–88 season was a stellar one, as he garnered a dozen goals and assists. Those numbers weren't quite good enough to capture the Norris Trophy, though. Who edged him out for the award given to the league's top defenseman?

Q55 What award did the goaltending duo of Al Jensen and Pat Riggin win at the end of the 1983–84 season?

Q56 In what hockey-related business did Dave Christian's father and uncle make their fortune?

Q57 This forward joined the Caps as a free agent after playing on the U.S. Olympic Team in 1984. He is a naturalized American citizen and a graduate of Boston College. Name him.

Q58 In a 1985 swap of goaltenders, Washington obtained Pete Peeters from the Bruins for Pat Riggin. What team originally drafted Peeters in 1977?

Q59 On November 18, 1992, Reggie Savage scored his first NHL goal on a penalty shot. Against what goalie did Savage score?

Q60 Reggie Savage scored his first NHL goal on a penalty shot. Name the three players who preceded the Capital winger in netting their inaugural NHL goal in this manner.

Q61 Who was the first-ever Cap representative in the All-Star Game?

WASHINGTON CAPITALS

A49 Montreal Canadiens (1975–76—1981–82)
Hartford Whalers (1985–86—1987–88)

A50 Atlanta Flames
Calgary Flames

A51 Birmingham Bulls

A52 Rick Green (1976–82)

A53 He was the first American to win the trophy.

A54 Ray Bourque

A55 The Jennings Trophy (fewest goals against)

A56 They created the Christian Brothers Hockey Stick company.

A57 Gary Sampson

A58 Philadelphia Flyers

A59 Minnesota's Jon Casey

A60 St. Louis Eagle Ralph Bowman (1934)
L.A. King Phil Hoene (1973)
Philadelphia Flyer Ilkka Sinisalo (1981)

A61 Denis Dupere

Q62 Who was the first Cap to be selected for a starting position in the NHL All-Star Game?

Q63 Who is the only Washington goalie to appear in an NHL All-Star Game?

Q64 Who earned MVP honors at the 1981 All-Star Game thanks to his performance between the pipes?

Q65 As of 1991–92, which Cap players have been selected to the first team of the NHL All-Star Team?

Q66 Who was the first Washington goalie to garner an assist?

Q67 Who was the first Cap to be named NHL Player of the Week?

Q68 Who was the first Cap to have his jersey retired by the team?

Q69 Who scored the Capitals' first-ever goal?

Q70 The Caps set a club record for consecutive winning games on January 27, 1984, with a 6–1 drubbing of Toronto. How long did the streak last?

Q71 In 1974–75, the Caps set a dubious league record: fewest wins on the road. How many did they garner away from the friendly confines of the Cap Centre?

Q72 Who was the first Cap to record a hat trick?

Q73 Who was the first Cap to score five goals in a game?

Q74 Who set a team record as the first player to bag a goal against every NHL team in one season (1981–82)?

Q75 Washington set an NHL record in 1980 (since surpassed) for the fastest two goals from the start of a period by one team. What two Capitals scored within 30 seconds of the start of the second period?

Q76 Which Cap was the first American-born player to net 30 goals in a season?

Q77 What pair of players have scored three goals each in a playoff game?

Q78 The Capitals once netted 12 goals in a game to achieve a lopsided victory. Who did they pummel by a 12–2 score at home?

Q79 Who was the first Cap to notch 60 goals and 100 points in a season?

WASHINGTON CAPITALS

A62   Mike Gartner (1981)

A63   Pat Riggin (1983–84; second team. Al Jensen was selected the same year, but was injured and did not play.)

A64   Mike Liut

A65   Rod Langway (1982–83; 1983–84)
Scott Stevens (1987–88)

A66   Michel Belhumeur (on Bruce Cowick's goal; March 20, 1975, against Minnesota)

A67   Gerry Meehan (1976–77)

A68   Yvon Labre

A69   Jim Hrycuik (vs. the Rangers' Ed Giacomin, 1974–75)

A70   10 games (ending with a 4–3 loss to the Jets on February 19, 1984)

A71   One

A72   Ron Lalonde (against Detroit on March 30, 1974)

A73   Bengt Gustafsson (vs. Philadelphia; 1983–84)

A74   Dennis Maruk

A75   Mike Gartner (0:08)
Bengt Gustafsson (0:30)
(January 27, 1980: vs. N.Y. Islanders)

A76   Tom Rowe

A77   Dino Ciccarelli (vs. New Jersey; April 5, 1990)
John Druce (vs. Rangers; April 21, 1990)

A78   Quebec Nordiques (February 6, 1990)

A79   Dennis Maruk (1981–82: 60 goals, 136 points)

Q1   Which player set a franchise record for most goals by a rookie, with 32?

Q2   Which Cap was the youngest player (age 20) and first rookie to be named the team MVP in franchise history?

Q3   Who has the dubious distinction of taking the first penalty by a Cap skater?

Q4   Which Washington enforcer committed the biggest Capital offense when he put his name in the team record books with 207 penalty minutes during one campaign?

Q5   Who was the first Cap to attempt two penalty shots in one season?

Q6   Who was the first Cap to bag a goal on a penalty shot?

Q7   He was the first player to reach the 100-point plateau in a Washington uniform. Name him.

Q8   Who set a team mark for points in a game when he potted four goals and three assists in a game against Hartford on March 18, 1989?

Q9   Which Cap set a team record for rookies when he bagged five points in a 1981 game against Philadelphia?

Q10   The team's first year in the NHL was one to forget, as they set league lows for fewest wins and most losses in a season. How long did the Caps' longest losing streak last?

Q11   During the 1982–83 season, the Caps set the club mark for their longest undefeated streak. What is the record?

Q12   What is the Caps' longest win streak?

Q13   The most single-season points ever registered by the club was 107 (50 wins, 7 ties). In what campaign did the Caps reach this zenith?

Q14   What is the club record for ties in a season?

WASHINGTON CAPITALS

A1   Bob Carpenter (1981–82)

A2   Mike Gartner

A3   Bill Mikkelson (for hooking against the Rangers; October 9, 1974)

A4   Gord Lane (1976–77)

A5   Bengt Gustafsson (January 5, 1980: at Minnesota; unsuccessful vs. Gilles Meloche
February 5, 1980: at L.A.; unsuccessful vs. Ron Grahame)

A6   Steve Atkinson (February 1, 1974; vs. Vancouver's Ken Lockett)

A7   Gerry Meehan (He hit the century mark on November 9, 1977.)

A8   Dino Ciccarelli

A9   Greg Theberge

A10   17 games

A11   14 games (November 24, 1982–December 23, 1982: 9 wins and 5 ties)

A12   10 games (January 27, 1984–February 18, 1984)

A13   1985–86

A14   18 (1980–81)

GLORY DAYS

Q1   What NHL career playoff record did Dale Hunter establish?

Q2   Who put his name in the record books when he recorded the Capitals' first-ever playoff goal?

Q3   Name the netminder who has bragging rights for most victories (7) in postseason play for the Caps.

Q4   The Capitals missed qualifying for the playoffs by the same margin in consecutive seasons, 1979–80 and 1980–81. By how many points did the team miss the opportunity for postseason glory in each of the two campaigns?

Q5   Who did the Capitals face off against in the team's first-ever playoff series?

Q6   Who led the Caps in scoring with five goals in four games in the team's first-ever playoff series in 1982–83?

Q7   The New York Islanders edged the Caps four games to three in the first round of the 1986–87 playoffs. Which Isle scored the winning goal at 8:47 of the fourth overtime of the seventh game?

Q8   What Cap saved the day when he fired in the game-winning goal in OT of Game 7 against the Flyers in the 1987–88 Patrick Division semifinals?

Q9   After dropping the first game to the Rangers in 1989–90, the Caps stormed back to win four straight games on the strength of John Druce's scoring. What team eliminated the Caps in four straight to take the Wales Conference Finals crown?

Q10   What player garnered a team-high 11 points—all assists—in the 1992 playoffs?

TRADES, WAIVES, AND ACQUISITIONS

Q1   The Capitals acquired Ron Lalonde and Don Seiling in a late 1974 deal with Pittsburgh. Who went to the Steel City in return?

Q2   Who was the first player taken in the team's initial Amateur Draft?

Q3   A first-round draft choice by the Penguins, this veteran blueliner came to Washington via Detroit in a 1975 exchange for Dave Kryskow. Name him.

WASHINGTON CAPITALS

A1   Most playoff penalty minutes of any player in NHL history (As of the 1992–93 season, he is still adding to his record total.)

A2   Bob Gould (1983)

A3   Pete Peeters (1988)

A4   One

A5   New York Islanders (1982–83; New York took the series, 3–1.)

A6   Bob Gould

A7   Pat LaFontaine (at 1:58 A.M.; final score: 3–2. The game was the fifth longest in league history.)

A8   Dale Hunter

A9   Boston Bruins

A10   Mike Ridley

A1   Lew Morrison

A2   Greg Joly (1974)

A3   Jack Lynch

TRADES, WAIVES, AND ACQUISITIONS

Q4 Don McLean and this centerman came to the Caps for a number one pick in a deal with the Flyers. Who came to the Caps in the 1975 deal with Philly?

Q5 Who was the first player chosen overall in the 1976 Amateur Draft?

Q6 Who did Washington send packing when the team acquired Bob Girard and a draft choice in a late 1977 trade with Cleveland?

Q7 A junior hockey linemate of Wayne Babych and Brent Peterson, this winger was the Caps' first choice in the second round of the 1978 draft. Who is he?

Q8 Dubbed the "All-American Trade," Tom Rowe was swapped to the Whalers for this Minnesota native in a January 1979 deal. Identify the player who came to Washington in the transaction.

Q9 Name the blueliner the Caps acquired in exchange for Mike Kaszyki in a February 1980 deal with the Maple Leafs.

Q10 Mike Palmateer became a Capital when Tim Coulis and this blueliner were dispatched to Toronto. Name the player who was sent north of the border in the 1980 deal.

Q11 Who was added to the Calgary roster when the Capitals traded for Bob Gould and Randy Holt in a 1981 transaction with the Flames?

Q12 After he had appeared in only one game for Detroit, the Caps received this player when they shipped Mark Lofthouse to the Wings in a 1981 trade. Who came to the nation's capital in the deal?

Q13 The Caps pulled off a blockbuster deal when they shipped Rick Green and Ryan Walter north of the border in a 1982 deal with the Canadiens. Who came to D.C.?

Q14 In a straight-up deal with Quebec, the Capitals dispatched Tim Tookey to Quebec in exchange for this American-born defenseman. Who came to D.C. in the 1982 trade with the Nordiques?

Q15 A first-round draft choice of the Atlanta Flames, this defenseman was traded to Washington from the Maple Leafs in 1983 for Lee Norwood. Who was he?

Q16 What blueliner came to the Caps in return for Brian Engblom and Ken Houston in a 1983 swap with Los Angeles?

WASHINGTON CAPITALS

A4   Bill Clement

A5   Rick Green (1976: first pick overall)

A6   Walt McKechnie

A7   Paul Mulvey

A8   Alan Hangsleben

A9   Pat Ribble

A10   Robert Picard

A11   Pat Ribble

A12   Al Jensen

A13   Brian Engblom
Doug Jarvis
Craig Laughlin
Rod Langway

A14   Lee Norwood

A15   Dave Shand

A16   Larry Murphy

TRADES, WAIVES, AND ACQUISITIONS

Q17   On October 4, 1983, the Caps acquired Greg Adams in return for Torrie Robertson. With what team did they do business?

Q18   On March 12, 1985, the Capitals picked up Mark Taylor in exchange for Jim McGeough. With what team did Washington wheel and deal?

Q19   Who came to Washington when the Caps shipped Dean Evason and Peter Sidorkiewicz to Hartford in 1985?

Q20   Who did the Capitals acquire when they sent Doug Jarvis packing in a late 1985 trade with Hartford?

Q21   Identify the pair of players who came from the Motor City when Washington dealt Darren Veitch to Detroit in a 1986 transaction with the Red Wings.

Q22   In a New Year's Day blockbuster trade, the Capitals sent Bob Carpenter and a draft choice to the Rangers in return for a trio of players. Who came to Washington from the Big Apple in the 1987 transaction?

Q23   When Gaetan Duchesne and Alan Haworth were sent north of the border, the Caps acquired Dale Hunter and a netminder. What goalie was included in the 1987 deal with the Quebec Nordiques?

Q24   What rear guard came to the Caps in exchange for Al Jensen in a 1987 trade with the L.A. Kings?

Q25   Ed Kastelic and Grant Jennings were dealt to Hartford for Mike Millar and a defenseman. Who else was dealt to the Caps in the summer of '88 trade?

Q26   What well-traveled defenseman came to the Capitals from the Kings in 1988 for Craig Laughlin?

Q27   A total of four NHLers were involved in the deal that brought Dino Ciccarelli to Washington in 1989. What other players changed uniforms in the transaction with Minnesota?

Q28   Name the tandem that shuffled off to Buffalo when the Caps traded for Calle Johansson in a 1989 swap with the Sabres.

Q29   Who did the Capitals obtain when they shipped Yvon Corriveau to the Whalers on March 5, 1990?

Q30   Who came to Washington in return for Steve Maltais and Trent Klatt in a June 1991 transaction with Minnesota?

WASHINGTON CAPITALS

A17   Hartford Whalers

A18   Pittsburgh Penguins

A19   David Jensen

A20   Jorgen Pettersson

A21   John Barrett
Greg Smith

A22   Kelly Miller
Bob Crawford
Mike Ridley

A23   Clint Malarchuk

A24   Garry Galley

A25   Neil Sheehy

A26   Grant Ledyard

A27   Ciccarelli and Bob Rouse came to the Caps for Mike Gartner and Larry Murphy.

A28   Clint Malarchuk
Grant Ledyard

A29   Mike Liut

A30   Shawn Chambers

TRADES, WAIVES, AND ACQUISITIONS

Q31 In an encore appearance, the Caps brought Yvon Corriveau back to the team in a 1992 deal with Hartford. How was the winger originally acquired by the team seven years earlier?

Q32 In a swap of right wingers, the Caps acquired Pat Elynuik in exchange for John Druce early in the 1992–93 season. With what team did the Caps do business?

Q33 During the 1992–93 season, the Capitals picked up defenseman Paul Cavallini from the Blues. Who did Washington send to St. Louis in the deal?

WASHINGTON CAPITALS

A31   Corriveau was the Caps' first-round draft choice in 1985.

A32   Winnipeg Jets

A33   Kevin Miller

*** FAST FACTS ***

NHL SEASON RECORDS SET BY THE CAPS IN THE 1974–75
SEASON—
    Fewest Points (minimum 70 games): 21
    Fewest Wins: 8
    Most Goals Against: 446
    Most Losses: 67
    Most Home Losses: 28
    Most Road Losses: 39
    Fewest Road Wins: 1
    Longest Losing Streak: 17 (February 18, 1975—March 26, 1975)
    Longest Home Losing Streak: 11 (February 18, 1975—March 30, 1975)
    Longest Road Losing Streak: 37 (October 9, 1974—March 26, 1975)

When Terry Murray succeeded Yvon Labre as the team's assistant coach in 1982–83 and teamed up with his older brother, Bryan, it marked the first-ever combination of coaching brothers in the annals of the league.

It was defense with a capital D in the 1983–84 season, as the Capitals led the NHL in team defense, penalty killing, and shutouts.

The Capital Centre was the first arena in the United States with fully computerized ticketing.

In 1991–92, the Caps posted the best divisional mark with an incredible .643 winning percentage achieved against a group of teams that collectively finished 51 games above .500.

An Unlikely Hero—John Druce's 1989–90 Playoff Records:
    Most Goals (14)
    Most Power-Play Goals (8)
    Game-Winning Goals (4)
    Points (17)

Washington Redskins

WASHINGTON REDSKINS

THE 1982 WASHINGTON REDSKINS
SUPER BOWL XVII CHAMPIONS

THE SUITS

Q1   How many head coaches have directed the Washington Redskins?

Q2   Who has the best win-loss percentage among all Redskin coaches?

Q3   Who has the worst win-loss percentage among Redskin coaches?

Q4   Who was the first Washingtonian to be named head coach of the Redskins?

Q5   What Washington head coach was fired on the evening of the last game of the season?

Q6   The Redskins' first coach was at the helm from 1937 to 1942. Who was he?

Q7   In what business was George Marshall involved when he became part-owner of the NFL's Boston Braves in 1932?

Q8   George Marshall is credited with bringing two entertainment features to the NFL. What are they?

Q9   What two offensive innovations did Ray Flaherty introduce to the NFL as coach of the Redskins?

Q10   Ray Flaherty left the Skins following their victory in the 1942 NFL championship game. Where did he spend the next three seasons?

Q11   Ray Flaherty coached two other clubs after he left Washington in 1942. Name the teams he took control of.

WASHINGTON REDSKINS

A1   17

A2   Ray Flaherty (47–16–3, .735)

A3   Herman Ball (4–16, .200)

A4   Adm. John Whelchel

A5   Mike Nixon (The Skins had just finished losing a game on December 18, 1960, when he was given the ax. The club had a 1–9–2 record that year.)

A6   Ray Flaherty

A7   He was operating a laundry in Washington, D.C.

A8   A team band
The halftime show

A9   The behind-the-line screen pass
The two-platoon system for offense and defense

A10   In the U.S. Navy

A11   New York Yankees (1946–48)
Chicago Hornets (1949)
(Both teams were in the All-American Football Conference.)

Q12   John Whelchel's Redskin coaching career came to an abrupt end on November 7, 1949, when, by mutual agreement, his contract was canceled. What was the club's record up to that point in the season?

Q13   Dick Todd became the Washington head coach before the 1951 season was four games old. Who was dismissed after an 0–3 start that year?

Q14   After firing his winless coach three games into the 1951 season, George Marshall turned to a Chicago assistant coach to lead his Redskins. Unfortunately, Papa Bear George Halas refused to part with the man unless he received a Washington star (killing the deal). Name the two men in such demand.

Q15   Curly Lambeau came to the Redskins in 1952 with 33 straight years of experience as a head coach, 31 of them with the Green Bay Packers. Where were the other two seasons spent?

Q16   What was Curly Lambeau's given name?

Q17   Joe Kuharich was permitted to leave the Redskins after five seasons so that he could assume a similar position in collegiate football. At what school did he become head coach?

Q18   Mike Nixon was known as "Jock's Boy" or "Little Jock" around the gridiron. Who was the "Jock" to whom the nickname refers?

Q19   Jack Kent Cooke's fortunes began in the streets of Hamilton, Ontario. What did he sell in his Canadian hometown?

Q20   Jack Kent Cooke's first venture into professional sports began with his acquisition of a minor league baseball team in 1951. What was that club?

Q21   Jack Kent Cooke built the first privately funded indoor arena in the United States in three decades. What is the name of his facility?

Q22   Bill McPeak was an All-Pro defensive end in the NFL. With what club did he spend his entire nine-year playing career?

Q23   Otto Graham was a starting guard on Northwestern University's basketball team. With what hoops Hall of Famer did he play on at squad?

Q24   Otto Graham was the first professional to play in two sports. Name the clubs he suited up for.

Q25   What was the nickname of the line on which Vince Lombardi played while a member of the Fordham football team?

WASHINGTON REDSKINS

A12   3–3–1 (Ironically, the resignation came the day after a Washington victory; the Redskins finished the season with a 4–7–1 record.)

A13   Herman Ball

A14   Chicago assistant coach: Hunk Anderson
Player wanted by Halas: Paul Lipscomb

A15   Chicago Cardinals (1950–51)

A16   Earl

A17   Notre Dame

A18   Dr. John Bain "Jock" Sutherland (Sutherland was head coach at the University of Pittsburgh, under whom Nixon played and coached for 12 years.)

A19   Encyclopedias

A20   Toronto Maple Leafs

A21   The Forum (home of the Los Angeles Kings and Lakers)

A22   Pittsburgh Steelers

A23   George Mikan

A24   Cleveland Browns (NFL)
Rochester Royals (NBA)

A25   "The Seven Blocks of Granite"

Q26 What Hall of Famer played alongside of Vince Lombardi on the Fordham defensive line?

Q27 Vince Lombardi produced a motivational film that is still in great demand. What is the title of the film?

Q28 Vince Lombardi coached the Skins for a single season—1969—before he succumbed to cancer. How old was Lombardi at the time of his death?

Q29 At what two colleges did George Allen coach before he entered the NFL coaching ranks?

Q30 George Allen came to Washington in 1971 with five years of head coaching experience, all with the same NFL club. What team did he abandon to come to D.C.?

Q31 In his first year with Washington, George Allen had four assistant coaches on his staff who had been or would later become head coaches in the NFL. Who were they?

Q32 Of the seven seasons that George Allen was head coach of the Redskins, how many of them were winning ones?

Q33 Jack Pardee retired from the playing field in 1965 for one season. What made him temporarily leave the gridiron?

Q34 Jack Pardee's head coaching debut was made during the 1974 season. With what franchise was he associated?

Q35 Who did Jack Pardee coach immediately prior to arriving in D.C. in 1978?

Q36 Joe Gibbs was an assistant coach in the NFL with three different teams. Name the clubs.

Q37 Joe Gibbs was a 1976 national champion. In what sport did he excel?

Q38 When Joe Gibbs was selected as head coach of the Redskins in 1981, he was an assistant coach with another team. With what team was he under contract at the time?

Q39 Who was the first of Joe Gibbs's assistant coaches to leave the club to become a head coach with another NFL team?

Q40 Joe Gibbs is one of three NFL coaches to have won three or more Super Bowls. Who are the other two?

WASHINGTON REDSKINS

A26   Alex Wojciechowicz

A27   "Second Effort"

A28   57

A29   Morningside (Iowa)
Whittier (California)

A30   Los Angeles Rams

A31   Ted Marchibroda
Charley Winner
Marv Levy
Mike McMormack

A32   All seven

A33   He had an operation to remove cancer in his arm. (He resumed his career
in 1966 and played another seven years.)

A34   Florida (Orlando) Blazers
(of the World Football League)

A35   Chicago Bears (1975–77)

A36   St. Louis Cardinals
Tampa Bay Buccaneers
San Diego Chargers

A37   Racquetball

A38   San Diego Chargers

A39   Dan Henning (1982: Atlanta Falcons)

A40   Chuck Noll (4)
Bill Walsh (3)

THE SUITS

Q41   How many losing seasons did Washington have under Joe Gibbs during his twelve year tenure?

Q42   Charlie Casserly was originally "hired" by George Allen in 1977 as an intern for the Redskins. What was the future general manager's profession prior to arriving in D.C.?

Q43   Assistant coach Jim Hanifan played only one year of professional football. With what team did he take the field?

Q44   Richie Pettibon joined the Skins as an assistant coach in 1978 and remained with the club into the 1990s. With what NFL team did he first hold an assistant's position?

Q45   At what college was Richie Pettibon an all-conference quarterback?

Q46   Name the three teams that Richie Pettibon played on from 1959 to 1972.

Q47   How many Pro Bowl appearances did Richie Pettibon make during his playing career?

THE UNIFORMS

Q1   Who was the first native Washingtonian to sign a contract with the Redskins?

Q2   What halfback retired from football immediately after the season in which he won the NFL rushing title?

Q3   Who was the first player in NCAA history to pass for over 5,000 yards (5,447) and rush for over 3,000 (3,335) during his collegiate career?

Q4   This Redskin was the first safety in NFL history to be selected to the consensus All-Pro team in his first two years in the league. Name him.

Q5   Name the Redskin defensive back who once finished fifth in Heisman Trophy voting—the highest finish ever by a college defensive back.

Q6   This Redskin was the first native-born Alaskan to play in the NFL. Name him.

WASHINGTON REDSKINS

A41   One (1988: 7–9)

A42   He was a high school teacher-football coach in Massachusetts.

A43   Toronto Argonauts (of the Canadian Football League)

A44   Houston Oilers (1974–77)

A45   Tulane

A46   Chicago Bears (1959–1968)
         Los Angeles Rams (1969–1970)
         Washington Redskins (1971–1972)

A47   Four

--- · ---

A1   Albert "Dugie" DuGoff (He was cut before he ever played a regular-season game with the team.)

A2   Cliff Battles

A3   Brian Mitchell

A4   Paul Krause (1964 and 1965)

A5   Terry Hoage (in the 1983 balloting)

A6   Mark Schlereth

Q7   What Redskin was the first black to play collegiate football for the Alabama Crimson Tide?

Q8   Name the player who, after being traded from the Redskins, was permanently banned from professional football for accepting a bribe to throw a game.

Q9   What was the first father-and-son combination to play in the NFL?

Q10   What Redskin ran 83 yards for a touchdown with an opening preseason game kickoff the first time he touched a football in his NFL career?

Q11   Which Redskin was the first to ever be awarded the Ernie Davis Memorial Award (MVP) at the Coaches' All-American Game?

Q12   This Redskin started at guard in Washington's first game, and died eight years later from wounds suffered in battle during World War II. Name him.

Q13   Six members of the 1937 world champion Washington Redskins are in the Football Hall of Fame. Name them.

Q14   Who scored all of the Redskins' points in the first game ever played by the franchise after its move to Washington?

Q15   Who led the Redskins in receiving yards in their first season in Washington?

Q16   Who was the first player to sign a contract with the new Washington Redskin franchise?

Q17   How many seasons did Hall of Famer Cliff Battles play in the NFL?

Q18   How many times during his career did Cliff Battles lead the NFL in rushing?

Q19   Why did Cliff Battles abandon football at the peak of his career?

Q20   Slingin' Sammy Baugh went to Texas Christian on a baseball scholarship and had signed with a big league team by the time George Marshall offered him an NFL pact. With what baseball team had Baugh inked a deal?

Q21   In his senior year, Sammy Baugh led the College All-Stars to victory over the NFL 1936 champions. Who did he and his fellow collegians defeat?

WASHINGTON REDSKINS

A7   Wilbur Jackson (1971–73)

A8   Frank Filchock (While playing for the Giants, he was accused of taking a bribe to throw the 1946 championship game.)

A9   Frank "Tiger" Walton (1934–35—1944–45)
Joe Walton (1957–60)
(Both wore Number 21 with the Redskins.)

A10   Dick James (August 17, 1956: vs. the Rams)

A11   Pat Richter (1962)

A12   Eddie Kahn

A13   George Preston Marshall (owner)
Ray Flaherty (coach)
Sammy Baugh (quarterback)
Cliff Battles (running back)
Turk Edwards (tackle)
Wayne Millner (end)

A14   Riley Smith (Smith kicked two field goals, returned an interception for a touchdown, and kicked the extra point.)

A15   Charley Malone (28 catches, 419 yards)

A16   Sammy Baugh (1937)

A17   Six (1932–37)

A18   Twice (1933 and 1937)

A19   He left football to make more money. (His salary was frozen at $3,000 and he resented the attention and money given to teammate Sammy Baugh. He went on to form his own company and became a millionaire.)

A20   St. Louis Cardinals

A21   Green Bay Packers

Q22 In order to entice Sammy Baugh to play for the Redskins, the club offered him a signing bonus to ink his name on a contract. How much did that bonus pay?

Q23 In 1937, Sammy Baugh signed deals with two professional sports teams. The Redskins were one. What was the other?

Q24 On August 2, 1938, Sammy Baugh made a major career announcement, much to the elation of the Redskin club. What was Sammy's decision?

Q25 A picture of Sammy Baugh sitting on the bench during the 1943 NFL title game won a number of national awards. What is Baugh doing in the picture?

Q26 Sammy Baugh was ejected from just one game in his entire 16-year career. With whom did the Redskin quarterback fight, leading to the ejection?

Q27 At what college did Sammy Baugh take an assistant coach's position, immediately after retiring from Washington in 1952?

Q28 Sammy Baugh is considered one of the greatest quarterbacks in NFL history. In what category does he still hold league records?

Q29 Sammy Baugh respected this friend and teammate so much that he named one of his sons after the Redskin running back. Who was Baugh's buddy?

Q30 In what bizarre fashion did Turk Edwards's career end in a 1940 game against the Giants?

Q31 Nicknamed "Little Indian," this Redskin played so vigorously that he suffered more broken bones than any other player in NFL history. Name him.

Q32 Name the Redskin quarterback who was a direct descendant of the Confederate general Braxton Bragg.

Q33 Bob Goode rushed 107 yards through a Pittsburgh blizzard in the 1951 season finale, but missed the ground-gaining championship by a mere 14 yards. Name the Giant who edged him out.

Q34 Charley "Choo-Choo" Justice played in 1950 and from 1952 through 1954. The All-American retired in 1951 to take an assistant coaching job. For what college did Justice temporarily interrupt his career?

WASHINGTON REDSKINS

A22 $500

A23   Baseball's St. Louis Cardinals

A24   Baugh decided to abandon his baseball career and concentrate on football.

A25   He is shown crying.

A26   Cardinal Don Joyce (September 28, 1952: the Skins' season opener)

A27   Hardin-Simmons University

A28   Punting (highest career average—45.10 yards—and highest average in a season—51.40 yards in 1940)

A29   Dick Todd

A30   After Edwards and Mel Hein participated in the pregame coin-toss ceremony. Edwards turned toward the Washington bench. He caught his spike in the turf, his knee gave way, and his career ended.

A31   Wilbur Moore

A32   "Hurlin' Harry" Gilmer

A33   Eddie Price

A34   North Carolina (under Carl Snavely)

Q35   Drafted by Washington in 1951 in the 17th round, this Redskin played both offense and defense for three seasons. After jumping to the CFL for one year, he came back and was solely used as a defensive end until traded to the Rams in 1959. Name this five-time Pro Bowler.

Q36   Ralph Guglielmi was the runner-up in the voting for the 1953 Heisman Trophy. Who beat him out that year?

Q37   When Vic Janowicz won the Heisman Trophy in 1950, he was the third recipient to ever win the honor while in his junior year of college. Who were the first two third-year men to be given the Heisman?

Q38   Vic Janowicz played two years of pro baseball before he joined the Skins in 1954. In what team's organization did he go to bat?

Q39   In 1957, the Redskins utilized three rookie running backs to carry the ball. Name the "Papoose Platoon."

Q40   Joe Walton set a club record in 1958 for first-season ends with 32 catches, 532 yards, and 5 TDs, but that was not his first year with Washington. What position did Walton primarily play in his rookie (1957) year?

Q41   Name the player who was once selected as both offensive and defensive MVP, in a game against the Eagles on September 28, 1958.

Q42   What club selected Johnny Olszewski with its number one pick in the 1953 draft?

Q43   This player was presented a car by Richard Nixon when he left the Redskins and was the favorite pro player of the then vice president. Name him.

Q44   Andy Stynshula's hometown was the site of the first pro football game ever played. Where does the Redskin defensive end hail from?

Q45   Name the Washington receiver who set a club record (since surpassed) for single-season receptions with 53 in 1961, despite suffering a broken hand in the 11th game.

Q46   What club originally drafted George Izo with its first-round pick in the 1960 draft?

Q47   When Eddie LeBaron was traded in 1960, Washington picked up a 1961 first-round draft pick. Who did the club select with that choice?

Q48   In his very first play with the Redskins, Norm Snead connected on a 38-yard touchdown pass. Who was the receiver on the TD?

WASHINGTON REDSKINS

A35 Gene Brito

A36 Wisconsin's Alan Ameche

A37 Army's Doc Blanchard (1945)
Southern Methodist's Doak Walker (1948)

A38 Pittsburgh Pirates'

A39 Fullback Don Bosseler
Right halfback Jim Podoley
Left halfback Ed Sutton

A40 Defensive end

A41 Joni James (He played both safety and running back in some games during his career.)

A42 St. Louis Cardinals

A43 Gene Brito

A44 Latrobe, Pa. (On August 21, 1895, Latrobe beat neighboring town Jeannette, 12–0.)

A45 Fred Dugan

A46 St. Louis Cardinals

A47 Defensive tackle Joe Rutgens (University of Illinois)

A48 Bill Anderson (August 19, 1961: preseason game vs. Chicago)

Q49   Cleveland traded Bobby Mitchell to the Skins because the Browns were interested in Washington's draft rights to a collegiate running back. Who did the Lake Erie club covet?

Q50   Bobby Mitchell made his mark with the Washington Redskins as a wide receiver. What position did he play before he came to D.C.?

Q51   With whom did Bobby Mitchell share the MVP Award for the 1958 All-Star Game?

Q52   When Bobby Mitchell retired after the 1968 season, only one player ranked ahead of him in career receptions. Who was that?

Q53   Nicknamed "The Bomb," this two-year Redskin (1963 and 64) was a triple threat—a runner, passer, and field goal kicker. Name him.

Q54   What college did Charley Taylor attend?

Q55   At what position did Charley Taylor earn the NFL's Rookie of the Year honor in 1964?

Q56   Midway through the 1966 season, Charley Taylor switched to the position that would distinguish him in football history. Against what team were the Skins playing when Taylor permanently moved to wide receiver?

Q57   Charley Taylor caught his 634th career pass in the 1975 season finale to make him the NFL's all-time reception leader. Who was the club's opponent when Taylor broke the old record?

Q58   How many catches did Charley Taylor have in his career?

Q59   How many seasons did Charley Taylor lead the NFL in receptions?

Q60   Len Hauss did not start at center for his college team, but was moved there later in his collegiate career. What was his original position?

Q61   In his rookie season, Paul Krause led the NFL in interceptions. How many did he nab in 1964?

Q62   In his rookie year, Sam Huff warmed the Giants' bench until the starting middle linebacker went down with an injury. Whose mishap was the Hall of Famer's start in pro football?

Q63   At the age of 24, Sam Huff became the first NFL defensive player to adorn the cover of what national publication in 1959?

WASHINGTON REDSKINS

A49   Syracuse's Ernie Davis (The Browns used the Skins' pick to select Davis, but he died before he ever played a down.)

A50   Halfback

A51   Jim Ninowski

A52   Raymond Berry (Berry had 631 catches to Mitchell's 521.)

A53   Tommy Tracy

A54   Arizona State University

A55   Running back

A56   St. Louis Cardinals (Late in the first quarter, he shifted from the backfield to the split-end position.)

A57   Philadelphia Eagles (He surpassed the 633 reception total of Don Maynard.)

A58   649

A59   Two (1966: 72; 1967: 70)

A60   Fullback

A61   12

A62   Ray Beck's (With Huff doing such a superior job, Beck retired shortly afterward.)

A63   *Time*

Q64   Sam Huff asked to return in 1969 when he heard that Vince Lombardi had been named coach of the Redskins. After his one-year retirement (1968), he became a player-coach and assisted in training the linebackers. Name the linebacker coach who he worked with that season.

Q65   When Sam Huff retired, he ranked second in career interceptions by a linebacker. Who was the only man ahead of him at that position?

Q66   Sam Huff made the Pro Bowl six times during his career. How many of those came while he was playing with Washington?

Q67   What was the name of the television special that featured linebacker Sam Huff?

Q68   What is Sonny Jurgensen's real name?

Q69   At what college did Sonny Jurgensen play football?

Q70   Sonny Jurgensen was the runner-up for the 1966 NFL passing title. Who edged him out for the QB crown that year?

Q71   In 1967, Sonny Jurgensen set an NFL record by throwing for 3,747 yards over the course of the season. Whose record did he shatter?

Q72   How old was Sonny Jurgensen when he won his third NFL individual passing crown in 1974?

Q73   Of his 18 years in the NFL, how many seasons did Sonny Jurgensen spend with Washington?

Q74   Jerry Smith spent twelve outstanding seasons with the club as the Skins' tight end. Who did he replace in the starting lineup during the 1965 campaign?

Q75   Name the defensive back who, in a game against the Giants on November 27, 1966, intercepted three passes, returned one of them for a 60-yard touchdown, and recovered a fumble for another TD.

Q76   What school did placekicker Charley Gogolak attend?

Q77   In a 1965 college game against Cornell, Charlie Gogolak faced an unusual defense while attempting a 54-yard field goal. What did his opponents try against the long-distance kicker?

Q78   Charley Gogolak set a collegiate record when he kicked 50 consecutive extra points. Who held the previous mark of 44 straight PATs?

WASHINGTON REDSKINS

A64   Harland Svare

A65   Baltimore's Don Shinnick (36)

A66   One (1964)

A67   "The Violent World of Sam Huff"

A68   Christian Adolph Jurgensen III

A69   Duke University

A70   Green Bay's Bart Starr

A71   Giant Y. A. Tittle's (1963: 3,145 yards)

A72   40 years old

A73   11 (1964–74)

A74   Pres Carpenter

A75   Brig Owens

A76   Princeton University

A77   They formed a human pyramid. (The kick was successful.)

A78   His brother Pete Gogolak while playing at Cornell.

Q79   After 12 seasons with the Bears, Stan Jones asked Chicago to trade him to Washington. Why did he request the move after a dozen years in the Windy City?

Q80   What Redskin was the 1967 recipient of the Heisman Trophy?

Q81   In 1967, three Redskins finished 1, 2, and 4 in the league in receptions—the highest rankings to date by receivers on the same team. Name the Washington players in order of their ranking.

Q82   Sam Huff's injury during the ninth game of the 1967 season was serious enough to knock him out for the season and cause him to temporarily retire from the game. Who finished out the season as Washington's starting middle linebacker?

Q83   In the 1967 season opener against the Eagles, this Redskin rookie returned a kickoff 96 yards—the first time he ever touched the football in a regular-season NFL contest. Name him.

Q84   The 1968 season was not a banner running year for Washington. Who led the team in rushing for that season with only 399 yards?

Q85   When Gary Beban graduated from UCLA in 1968, he left school with the fifth-highest total offensive yards (5,358) in collegiate history. Name the four who, by NCAA records, accounted for more yardage than Beban.

Q86   The first-round selection of the Skins in the 1967 draft, this defensive back was an All-American and won every possible honor at the University of Oregon. Despite the accolades, he lasted only one season in the NFL. Who is he?

Q87   Mike Bragg was a two-sport pro when he was kicking for the Redskins. What other sport did the punter play?

Q88   Free agent Curt Knight was signed by Washington prior to the 1968 season and went on to lead the team in scoring for the next five years. What college did the 1971 Pro Bowl kicker graduate from?

Q89   This Washington QB played the last two years of his 13-year NFL career with the Redskins as a backup. He will be mostly remembered for leading Cleveland to the 1964 championship and handing off to Jim Brown. Who is he?

Q90   Larry Brown was the runner-up in balloting for the NFL's Rookie of the Year honor in 1969. Name the player who won the distinction.

WASHINGTON REDSKINS

A79   He wanted to play his final season (1966) near his home in Rockville, Maryland.

A80   QB Gary Beban (UCLA)

A81   Charley Taylor
Jerry Smith
Bobby Mitchell

A82   Ed Breding

A83   John Love

A84   Gerry Allen

A85   Brigham Young's Virgil Carter (6,354)
Drake's Johnny Bright (5,903)
SMU and Tulsa's Jerry Rhome (5,879)
Florida's Steve Spurrier (5,290)

A86   Jim "Yazoo" Smith

A87   Tennis

A88   U.S. Coast Guard Academy

A89   Frank Ryan

A90   Dallas's Calvin Hill

*** FAST FACTS ***

The Redskins were the first pro sports team to sell feature highlight films of games to the public. The club produced the 16mm, 21½-minute movie in 1948, and featured Skin highlights from the previous 11 seasons.

From 1952 to 1958, seven different players led the Redskins in rushing for the season. None of them led the team in ground yards before or after.

Redskin founder George Preston Marshall revolutionized the game of pro football with his innovations. He proposed the two-division system with a championship game, elaborate halftime shows, a Pro Bowl game, a slimmer football for better passing, and centering the play on the field.

Q91   When Larry Brown gained 4,177 rushing yards over his first four NFL seasons, he became only the third pro to reach the 4,000-yard plateau in that span of time. What two players preceded Brown in this accomplishment?

Q92   Larry Brown was the Redskins' leading rusher when he retired after the 1976 season with 5,875 career yards. Who was the club leader before Brown?

Q93   Where did Manny Sistrunk play collegiate ball?

Q94   Ron McDole played for three pro teams before he was acquired through a trade in 1970. Name his former clubs.

Q95   What was Ron McDole's nickname?

Q96   Two Redskins made three interceptions in one game during the 1971 season. Who were they?

Q97   He was the only receiver in the league to gain more than 1,000 yards in 1968 and 1969. In 1971, Washington acquired him in a trade for Cotton Speyrer and a first-round draft choice. Who was he?

Q98   George Allen imported three linebackers to the Redskins from the Rams in 1971. Name the trio of defenders.

Q99   What team chose Billy Kilmer in the first round of the 1961 draft?

Q100   Billy Kilmer had three nicknames. What were they?

Q101   From what club was Billy Kilmer acquired in 1971?

Q102   In order to acquire Billy Kilmer in 1971, Washington gave up fourth- and eighth-round draft picks in the 1972 draft. What player was also traded away for the quarterback?

Q103   With what team did Clifton McNeil win the NFL pass-receiving title in 1968?

Q104   Roy Jefferson played three different positions during his collegiate career at Utah. What were they?

Q105   Sam Wyche was with the Redskins for three seasons (1971–73). What were the quarterback's passing stats for those years?

WASHINGTON REDSKINS

A91 Jim Brown (5,055 yards)
Cookie Gilchrist (4,010)

A92 Don Bosseler (1957–64: 3,112 yards)

A93 Arkansas A & M

A94 St. Louis Cardinals
Houston Oilers
Buffalo Bills

A95 "The Dancing Bear"

A96 Jack Pardee
Richie Petitbone

A97 Roy Jefferson

A98 Maxie Baughan
Myron Pottios
Jack Pardee

A99 San Francisco 49ers

A100 "Furnace Face"
"Whiskey"
"Billy the Kid"

A101 New Orleans Saints

A102 Tom Russel

A103 San Francisco 49ers (71 receptions)

A104 Receiver
Running back
Placekicker

A105 0 attempts, 0 completions, 0 yards

THE UNIFORMS

Q106 Running back Tommy Mason made the rounds in the NFL, but his favorite crowd was in Nashville. What did the onetime Redskin do in the Tennessee city?

Q107 This Redskin never attended college, played with the semipro West Side Packers, and while in the Navy saw action with the Memphis Macs, before signing with Washington in 1972. Identify the player with the unusual background.

Q108 Name the Washington and St. Louis players who scored touchdowns in back-to-back kickoffs during a September 8, 1973 game.

Q109 Though he came from a small college, Duane Thomas shared his collegiate backfield for three seasons with another NFL star of the 1970s. What other pro came out of West Texas State?

Q110 Duane Thomas was a first-round pick of the Cowboys in 1970, with whom he played two seasons, and came to the Redskins in 1973. Between the time he played with the two NFC clubs, he was traded to two AFC teams, but he never played with either one. Name those American Conference clubs.

Q111 At what college did Ken Houston play his collegiate football?

Q112 What position did Ken Houston play while in college?

Q113 Ken Houston was finally replaced in the starting lineup in the sixth game of the 1980 season. Name the player who became the Redskins' starting safety that evening?

Q114 Deacon Jones started his Hall of Fame career with the Rams in 1961. In what round did L.A. draft the defensive end?

Q115 Joe Theismann was the runner-up in the 1970 balloting for the Heisman Trophy. Who won the honor that year?

Q116 What NFL team originally selected Joe Theismann in the 1971 draft?

Q117 What baseball club offered Joe Theismann a pro contract?

Q118 Though Joe didn't get into many games as a quarterback in his first two seasons with Washington, he did play another position with some regularity. In what role was Theismann used?

Q119 Joe Theismann's upgrade to permanent starter coincided with what change within the Redskin organization?

WASHINGTON REDSKINS

A106   He played at the Grand Ol' Opry. (Mason is an accomplished guitarist.)

A107   Herb Mul-key

A108   Cardinal Don Shy (97-yard return)
Redskin Herb Mul-Key (97-yard return)

A109   Mercury Morris

A110   New England
San Diego
(Dallas traded Thomas to the Patriots in 1972, but the running back refused to go and the deal was changed. He was later dealt to the Chargers, but didn't play for personal reasons.)

A111   Prairie View A & M

A112   Linebacker

A113   Tony Peters

A114   14th

A115   Jim Plunkett

A116   Miami Dolphins (Theismann opted for the CFL, and the Redskins traded their 1976 first-round draft pick to the Florida club in 1974 for his rights.)

A117   Minnesota Twins

A118   As a punt returner (In 1974 he returned 15 punts for 157 yards, and he returned two in 1975 for five yards.)

A119   Jack Pardee replaced George Allen as head coach.

Q120   Joe Theismann's first start as an NFL quarterback came two and a half years after he joined Washington. Who did he face in the fifth game of the 1976 season at RFK?

Q121   To what Redskin receiver did Joe Theismann complete his first NFL touchdown pass?

Q122   Joe Theismann had only one game in which he had 400-plus yards in total passing and rushing yards. Against what team did he reach his passing zenith?

Q123   Who caught the last TD pass thrown by Joe Theismann?

Q124   Mark Moseley came to Washington as a free agent in 1974 after previously leading two other clubs in scoring for a season. Where were the kicker's previous homes?

Q125   Whose career rushing record did John Riggins break while playing at Kansas?

Q126   John Riggins was originally selected with the sixth overall pick in the 1971 draft by the New York Jets. Name the five players chosen ahead of the Kansas running back.

Q127   On December 19, 1982, John Riggins became the fifth back in NFL history to exceed 2,000 carries. Name the four ball-carriers who preceded him.

Q128   John Riggins threw the first pass of his career during the 1983 NFC championship game. Who was on the receiving end of his 36-yard toss?

Q129   How many 1,000-yard rushing seasons did John Riggins have as a Redskin?

Q130   What is the highest number of 100-yard games that John Riggins had in a single season?

Q131   Only one player has more career rushing TDs than John Riggins. Who is he?

Q132   Name the three honorees who were inducted into the NFL Hall of Fame in 1992 along with John Riggins.

Q133   Who did John Riggins choose to present him for induction into the Hall of Fame?

WASHINGTON REDSKINS

A120   Kansas City Chiefs (K.C. won 33–30.)

A121   Charley Taylor (December 15, 1974)

A122   L.A. Raiders (October 2, 1983: The Redskins won 37–35.)

A123   Don Warren (November 19, 1985: vs. the Giants)

A124   Philadelphia
Houston

A125   Gale Sayers's

A126   1—Jim Plunkett (New England)
2—Archie Manning (New Orleans)
3—Dan Pastorini (Houston)
4—J. D. Hill (Buffalo)
5—Richard Harris (Philadelphia)

A127   Walter Payton
O. J. Simpson
Jim Brown
Franco Harris

A128   Charlie Brown

A129   Four

A130   Five (1984)

A131   Jim Brown (Brown has 106 to Riggo's 104.)

A132   Al Davis
Lem Barney
John Mackey

A133   NFL Commissioner Paul Tagliabue

Q134   Donnie Warren was the Redskins' first selection in the 1979 draft. In what round was Warren chosen?

Q135   In 1979, Rich Milot became the first rookie to start in a Redskin season opener in nine years. What veteran did he supplant as a starting linebacker?

Q136   Who punted for the Skins in the 1980 and 1981 seasons?

Q137   What is Art Monk's given name?

Q138   Art Monk was Washington's first-round pick in the 1980 draft. When was the last year prior to that that Washington had used its first-round choice to actually draft a player?

Q139   What was the name for the fans who avidly followed the career of Art Monk at RFK Stadium?

Q140   Art Monk missed the 1981 playoffs and Super Bowl XVII because of a broken foot, suffered in the last game of the regular season. Who was the opponent in that contest?

Q141   Art Monk caught 91 passes in 1985, but it was only second best in the league that season. Who led all NFL receivers that year?

Q142   Art Monk is one of four players to have more than 700 career receptions in the NFL. Who are the other three?

Q143   What club originally signed Jeff Bostic as a free agent out of college, but cut him during the 1980 training camp?

Q144   Mike Nelms was signed as a free agent in 1980 and immediately assumed punt-return responsibilities for the Redskins. In what year did Nelms call for his first fair catch?

Q145   This player earned the nickname "Frog" because of his leaping ability. He had a 33-inch vertical leap and led all players with a 35-foot-plus triple broad jump. Who is he?

Q146   Signed as a free agent in 1981, this wide receiver was the first Princeton player to ever have over 1,000 yards in receptions, and the first to ever gain over 1,000 yards in both rushing and receiving. Name him.

Q147   Dexter Manley has a cousin who also made his mark in the NFL. Who is his gridiron relative?

WASHINGTON REDSKINS

A134 Fourth

A135 Chris Hanburger

A136 Mike Connell

A137 James

A138 1968 (DB Jim Smith)

A139 The "Art Gallery"

A140 St. Louis Cardinals

A141 49er Roger Craig (92 receptions)

A142 Steve Largent
Charlie Joiner
James Lofton

A143 Philadelphia Eagles

A144 1984 (in the fourth game of the season)

A145 Clint Didier

A146 Cris Crissy

A147 Eric Dickerson

Q148   During the off-season, Dexter Manley became a public servant. What position did he assume in his community?

Q149   Though the city was home to his team's greatest adversary, Dexter Manley and his wife, Glinda, named their daughter Dalis after the Texas town. Why?

Q150   Since 1964, the Skins have had a total of three men play center. Name the trio of stalwarts.

Q151   What collegiate honor did Mark May win in his senior year?

Q152   After being drafted in 1981, Mark May was immediately thrust into the lineup after the starting left tackle retired at the beginning of training camp. Who did May replace on the line?

Q153   What is the name of the cookbook penned by Mark May?

Q154   Terry Metcalf played for St. Louis from 1973 through 1977, and was acquired by the Redskins in a 1981 trade. Where did the all-around back play from 1978 to 1980?

Q155   The "Fun Bunch" became national celebrities with their patented end zone celebration after each touchdown. Who originated the group?

Q156   In 1983, Charley Brown was one of a very "colorful" trio to be tied for the NFC lead in receptions. Who equaled the Redskin's catch total of 78 that year?

Q157   How did quarterback Tom Owens's inability to quite make his collegiate team cause him to become a three-year starter at the school?

Q158   Brigham Young quarterback Jim McMahon had a string of 152 passes without an interception during his collegiate career. Name the cornerback who ended McMahon's streak and was later drafted by the Redskins.

Q159   Three Washington linemen were selected to the 1983 NFC Pro Bowl squad. Name them.

Q160   What is "Babe" Laufenberg's real first name?

Q161   For all of his rookie year and the first game of the 1984 season, Charles Mann was on the second string. Who started at left end in front of Mann?

Q162   Darrell Green was clocked in at 10.08 for the 100 meters as a collegiate sprinter—the best time among all colleges and second best overall in the country. Who was the only American to register a better time in 1982?

WASHINGTON REDSKINS

A148   He was a Fairfax County deputy sheriff.

A149   Dexter was in Dallas when his wife called him to announce that she was pregnant.

A150   Len Hauss (1964–77)
Bob Kuziel (1978–80)
Jeff Bostic (1981–present)

A151   Outland Trophy (awarded to the nation's top interior lineman)

A152   Terry Hermeling

A153   "Mark May's Hog Cookbook"

A154   Toronto Argonauts (of the CFL)

A155   Rick Walker

A156   Ernest Gray
Roy Green

A157   Owens wasn't on the traveling squad of the Wichita State Shockers when the team's plane crashed, killing most of the school's football squad.

A158   Vernon Dean

A159   Jeff Bostic
Russ Grimm
Joe Jacoby

A160   Brandon (He was dubbed Babe by his older brother when they were children.)

A161   Todd Liebenstein

A162   Carl Lewis

Q18. Who did the Redskins trade in order to acquire "Johnny Oh" Olszewski from the Chicago Cardinals in 1958?

Q16. What was the given name of Curly Lambeau (second from left)?

Q23. In 1937, Sammy Baugh signed deals with two professional sports teams. The Redskins were one. What was the other franchise?

Q66. Sam Huff made the Pro Bowl six times during his career. How many of those came while he was playing with Washington?

Q163 Whose 1983 contract dispute forced Darrell Green into a Redskin starting spot that he never relinquished?

Q164 Jay Schroeder was selected by the Redskins in the third round of the 1984 draft. What two quarterbacks were taken ahead of the UCLA graduate?

Q165 With what pro baseball club did Jay Schroeder sign a contract and spend two seasons in the minors?

Q166 Gary Clark became a Redskin in 1985 after he signed on as a free agent. With what pro team did he begin his football career?

Q167 What is George Rogers's middle name?

Q168 George Rogers set an NFL rookie record in 1981 when he rushed for 1,674 yards. Who later surpassed Rogers's freshman mark?

Q169 Who recruited RC Thielemann for Arkansas University and influenced him to become a Razorback?

Q170 Clarence Verdin came to the Redskins through the USFL Supplemental Draft in 1986. With what team was Verdin playing in the failed league?

Q171 Kelvin Bryant was the fourth player in ACC history to rush for three 1,000-yard seasons. Who were the first three?

Q172 Kelvin Bryant started his pro football career in the USFL in 1983, and he established himself as the best runner in that league's short life. With what team did he play?

Q173 Kurt Gouvuea was the first person in Hawaii high school football history to be named MVP on both offense and defense by the media. What two positions did he play?

Q174 Mark Rypien is second in Washington State's history for single-season passing yardage (2,417). Who is first in the Cougars' record books?

Q175 In what round of the 1986 draft was Mark Rypien selected by Washington?

Q176 Mark Rypien hails from Spokane, Washington. Identify two other All-Stars from the sports world who call Spokane home.

Q177 Ricky Sanders began his pro football career in the USFL. For which team did he play in the now-defunct league?

WASHINGTON REDSKINS

A163   Jeris White's

A164   Boomer Esiason (Cincinnati)
Rick McIvor (St. Louis)

A165   Toronto Blue Jays

A166   Jacksonville Bulls (of the USFL)

A167   Washington (as in George Washington Rogers Jr.)

A168   Eric Dickerson

A169   Joe Gibbs (The Washington head coach was an assistant under Frank Broyles at the school.)

A170   Houston Gamblers

A171   Ted Brown
Amos Lawrence
Mike Voight

A172   Philadelphia Stars (In 1985, their final season, they became the Baltimore Stars.)

A173   Quarterback
Defensive back

A174   Jack Thompson (2,072 yards)

A175   Sixth (146th player overall)

A176   John Stockton—Utah Jazz
Ryne Sandberg—Chicago Cubs

A177   Houston Gamblers

Q178 Despite catching 101 passes in his rookie year, Ricky Sanders not only didn't lead the USFL in receptions, he was second on his team in catches. Who led with 115 grabs in 1984?

Q179 With what team did Doug Williams make his professional football debut in 1983?

Q180 In 1983, Doug Williams jumped the NFL ship and joined the new USFL. For what club did he quarterback in the fledgling league?

Q181 Doug Williams began the 1987 season on the bench but soon became the Redskins' starter for the balance of the year. How long did it take for Williams to enter his first game?

Q182 In 1991, Chip Lohmiller became the first player to outscore an entire team over a season since 1945. Name the NFL club that couldn't beat the 149 points totaled by the kicker.

Q183 What team selected Jim Lachey with the 12th overall pick in the 1985 draft?

Q184 Jim Lachey's crunching blow in Week 8 of the 1989 season was selected by *Sport* magazine as the Hit of the Year. Who absorbed the shock of Lachey's power in that hit?

Q185 Stan Humphries's hometown is Shreveport, Louisiana. Name the two former NFL quarterbacks who originated from that Bayou city.

Q186 What Redskin was the 1989 winner of the Outland Trophy (awarded to the nation's best interior lineman)?

Q187 Earnest Byner just missed putting his name in the Redskins' record books as the only player in team history to rack up 1,000 or more rushing yards in three straight seasons. By how many yards did Byner miss the mark?

Q188 Where was Earnest Byner baptized as a born-again Christian?

Q189 Fred Stokes was signed as a free agent in 1989 and became the starter later that season when the two players ahead of him at right end couldn't play. Name the two Redskins Stokes eventually replaced.

Q190 Martin Mayhew arrived in Washington as a Plan B acquisition in 1989. What club originally drafted the cornerback in the 10th round of the 1988 draft?

WASHINGTON REDSKINS

A178 Teammate Richard Johnson

A179 Tampa Bay Buccaneers

A180 Oklahoma Outlaws (which later became the Arizona Outlaws)

A181 Nine plays (Jay Schroeder injured his shoulder in the eighth play of the season opener against Philadelphia and Williams replaced him.)

A182 Indianapolis Colts (The Colts could only muster 145 points that year.)

A183 San Diego Chargers

A184 Raider Jerry Robinson

A185 Terry Bradshaw
Joe Ferguson

A186 Mo Elewonibi (while playing for Brigham Young)

A187 Two (He finished the 1992 season with 998 rushing yards.)

A188 In Darrell Green's Jacuzzi.

A189 Dexter Manley (suspended for drug use)
Markus Koch (injured)

A190 Buffalo Bills

Q191 On November 12, 1990, in a Monday night contest against the Eagles, both Jeff Rutledge and Stan Humphries went down with injuries. Who took over the signal-calling duties?

Q192 In 1990, Andre Collins became only the second rookie in the Joe Gibbs era to start every game in a season. Who was the first?

Q193 Alvoid Mays was signed as a free agent in May 1990 by Washington. What was Mays's profession when he was contacted by the club?

Q194 Jeff Rutledge was selected MVP of the 1978 Sugar Bowl. What team was he quarterbacking when he won the honor?

Q195 Jeff Rutledge is one of three players to participate in the Super Bowl with three different teams (Rams, Giants, and Redskins). Name the other two.

Q196 Mark Adickes was born in Banconstadt, Germany, and played his freshman year of football at Berlin American High School. What other future professional sports figure was a teammate of his?

Q197 Though selected in the first round of the NFL's 1984 supplemental draft, Mark Adickes chose not to sign with the Kansas City Chiefs. Where did the Baylor guard play his first two seasons of pro football?

Q198 Jason Buck has played in two Super Bowls. One was with the Skins in Super Bowl XXVI. With what other club did he participate in the postseason classic?

Q199 Terry Orr was signed by the Redskins in 1991 after the club lost one of its tight ends through free agency. Whose loss resulted in Orr's Super Bowl gain?

Q200 Identify the Redskin who had six knee operations during his college career, was the 263rd overall pick in the 1989 draft, and played in the Pro Bowl after the 1991 campaign.

Q201 Steve Gabbard was signed as a Plan B free agent in 1992 after he distinguished himself with the London Monarchs in the World League. What was the nickname of the offensive line on which he played in England?

WASHINGTON REDSKINS

A191 Running back Brian Mitchell (The Skins lost 28–14.)

A192 Darrell Green (1983)

A193 He was packing orange juice for Tropicana in Florida.

A194 Alabama Crimson Tide (over Ohio State)

A195 Matt Millen (Raiders, San Francisco, and Washington)
Preston Pearson (Baltimore, Pittsburgh, and Dallas)

A196 Pro baseball pitcher Danny Cox

A197 He played for the Los Angeles Express of the USFL.

A198 Cincinnati Bengals (Super Bowl XXIII)

A199 Ken Whisenhunt

A200 Mark Schlerth

A201 The "Nasty Boyz"

Q1 In what year did the Skins abandon the double-wing formation and adopt the new T-formation?

Q2 What was the Boston football franchise's original name?

Q3 In what year did the Boston Redskins move to the nation's capital?

Q4 Though the Browns won the game, Washington could boast that it held Hall of Famer Jim Brown to the lowest single-game rushing total of his career on November 30, 1958. How many yards did the team hold Brown to that day?

Q5 Where did the Redskins open the regular season in their first year in D.C.?

Q6 How many season-ticket holders did the Redskins have in their inaugural (1937) season?

Q7 Who threw out the first ball at the Washington Redskins' first home game in 1937?

Q8 The original Redskin band was an employees' band who asked permission to play at home games. What was the name of the musical group when it wasn't playing at the football games?

Q9 Who penned the words to the team's theme, "Hail to the Redskins," prior to the 1938 football season?

Q10 Who wrote the music to "Hail to the Redskins"?

Q11 "Hail to the Redskins" was the first pro football song ever to be sold on records. Who recorded the "Ballad for Battle" in 1939?

Q12 Since 1938, the Tribe has held training camp in seven different cities. Name them.

Q13 The Skins went 10–1 in the 1942 regular season and went on to win the NFL Championship. What was the only team to defeat Washington that year?

Q14 Washington was the first and only team in 1950 to announce that all of its out-of-town games would be televised. Who was the sponsor of this "extravagance"?

Q15 What announcer, who gained his fame by doing play-by-play in baseball, was the voice of the Redskins in the 1952 and 1953 seasons?

WASHINGTON REDSKINS

A1   1945

A2   Braves

A3   1937 (Approval of the franchise relocation was made on February 13 of that year.)

A4   12 (on 11 carries)

A5   Griffith Stadium

A6   958

A7   Jesse Owens

A8   Chestnut Farms' Dairy Employes Band

A9   Connie Griffith (wife of franchise owner George Preston Marshall)

A10   Maestro Barnee Breeskin

A11   Hal Kemp

A12   Anacostia, Maryland (1937)
Ballston, Virginia (1938)
Spokane, Washington (1939–40)
San Diego, California (1941–44)
Washington, D.C. (Georgetown University; 1945)
Occidental College, California (1946–62)
Carlisle, Pennsylvania (Dickinson College; 1963–present)

A13   New York Giants (New York won, 14–7, despite gaining only one yard rushing, completing only one pass, and not achieving a first down.)

A14   American Oil Company (Amoco)

A15   Mel Allen

Q16   Annual nemesis Dallas entered the NFL in 1960. What was the first year that the Redskins swept the regular-season series against the Cowboys?

Q17   What was the name of RFK Stadium when it first opened?

Q18   The first game in what is now RFK Stadium was held on October 1, 1961. Who ruined the facility's inauguration by handing Washington a 24–21 loss?

Q19   The Redskins finally tallied a home win in the last game of the 1961 season, when they prevailed by 10 points over an expansion team. Over what club did Washington triumph for its inaugural victory in RFK?

Q20   What was the first year in which the Redskins sold out all of their games in a season?

Q21   The Redskins defeated New Orleans on December 14, 1969, and ensured themselves a winning season. (They ended the year with a 7–5–2 record.) What season had been their last winning one prior to 1969?

Q22   One year after overtime was instituted in the NFL, the Skins played in their first five-quarter game. Who did Washington defeat 30–24 in that contest?

Q23   The Hogs were originated in 1982 to instill identity into a young Washington offensive line. Who is the author of this image?

Q24   The Redskins went 8–1 in the strike-shortened 1982 season. Who was the lone club to defeat Washington in its initial Super Bowl year?

Q25   The NFC standings were crowded in 1985, when four teams tied for the third-best regular-season record (10–6) in the conference. Name the clubs that had an identical record to Washington's.

Q26   The 1991 Redskins became only the sixth team in NFL history to register 17 or more wins in a single year. (They posted a 17–2 overall mark.) Name the five teams that Washington joined.

WASHINGTON REDSKINS

A16 1984

A17 D.C. Stadium

A18 New York Giants

A19 Dallas Cowboys

A20 1964

A21 1955

A22 Dallas Cowboys (November 2, 1975)

A23 Joe Bugel (the "Boss Hog")

A24 Dallas Cowboys

A25 Dallas Cowboys
New York Giants
San Francisco 49ers
(Because of the tie-breaker system, Washington was excluded from the playoffs.)

A26 1972 Miami Dolphins (17–0)
1984 San Francisco 49ers (18–1)
1985 Chicago Bears (18–1)
1978 Pittsburgh Steelers (17–2)
1986 New York Giants (17–2)

SETTING THE STANDARD

Q1   Only two players, both onetime Redskins, have ever won the NFL's version of the Triple Crown (leading the league in passing or running as well as interceptions and punting). Name the duo.

Q2   What is the club single-game record for first downs in a game?

Q3   Who set a team record by attempting 49 field goals in a season?

Q4   Mark Moseley was successful in 23 consecutive field goal attempts during the 1981 and 1982 seasons. Who is the only NFL kicker to have a longer streak of three-pointers?

Q5   Chip Lohmiller entered the NFL record books when he kicked field goals in 28 consecutive games—the second best such performance in the history of the league. With whom is he tied and who holds the record?

Q6   What is the longest winless streak the Redskins have ever suffered through?

Q7   The team the Redskins defeated to end their skein was also the last club they were victorious over before going winless. Name that club.

Q8   Who holds the record for games played in a Redskin uniform?

Q9   The greatest comeback in Redskin history occurred on November 28, 1965, when the club rebounded from a 21–0 deficit to register a 34–31 win. Who did Washington triumph over?

Q10   The "iron man" record for the Skins is 196 consecutive games. Who set this mark?

Q11   Nine of Ken Houston's interceptions were returned for TDs. Who held the previous NFL record of seven interceptions returned for touchdowns?

Q12   Who holds the club record for single-season interceptions?

Q13   Brig Owens is the career leader among Redskins for interceptions, with 36. Who ranks second in the club's history, with 31?

Q14   The longest interception return in the Redskins' history is 100 yards. Who holds the record?

Q15   Name the four Washington QBs who have led the NFL in passing.

Q16   Name the three QBs who have passed for more than 20,000 yards in their Washington career.

WASHINGTON REDSKINS

A1   Sammy Baugh (1943)
Bill Dudley (1946)

A2   39 (November 4, 1990: vs. Detroit; 14 rushing, 25 passing, 0 penalty)

A3   Curt Knight (1971; he was successful on 29 of them.)

A4   Chicago's Kevin Butler (24)

A5   Lohmiller is tied with Jim Turner. The record of 31 consecutive games with a successful field goal is held by Minnesota's Fred Cox.

A6   23 games (October 16, 1960 to December 17, 1961; the streak includes three tie games.)

A7   Dallas Cowboys (October 9, 1960 and December 17, 1961)

A8   Dave Butz (1975–88: 203)

A9   Dallas Cowboys

A10   Len Hauss (Hauss started 192 straight games, also a club record.)

A11   Herb Adderly

A12   Dan Sandifer (1948: 13)

A13   Sammy Baugh

A14   Barry Wilburn (November 26, 1987: vs. Minnesota)

A15   Sammy Baugh (1937, 1940, 1943, 1945, 1947, 1949)
Frank Filchock (1944)
Eddie Le Baron (1958)
Sonny Jurgensen (1967, 1969)

A16   Joe Theismann (25,206)
Sonny Jurgensen (22,585)
Sammy Baugh (22,085)

Q17 Which Washington quarterback once completed 87.5 percent of his passes in a game—the highest of any Skin QB with at least 15 attempts?

Q18 The highest single-season quarterback rating of any Redskin is 109.7. Who set this club record?

Q19 Which Redskin quarterback tossed 27 interceptions in one season and established a club record along the way?

Q20 The most TD passes tossed in one year by a Washington QB is 31. Who set this team mark?

Q21 Which Washington quarterback has the highest career completion percentage (minimum 1,000 attempts)?

Q22 Who holds the club single-season mark for passing yards?

Q23 What Redskin has the highest single-season completion percentage of any quarterback with a minimum of 150 attempts?

Q24 Name the Redskin kicker who set team records by attempting 10 PATs in a game and successfully hitting on nine of them.

Q25 Which Redskin holds the team record for appearances in the Pro Bowl as a Washington player?

Q26 Since 1960, only three who were not kickers have led the team in single-season scoring. Name them.

Q27 Mark Moseley holds the club record for scoring in consecutive games. What is his record?

Q28 Only two Redskins have ever scored four TDs in a game. Name them.

Q29 Who holds the single-season club record for points by a Redskin other than a kicker?

Q30 Who holds the club record for most career points as a Redskin other than a kicker?

Q31 In what season did the tribe set a NFL record by scoring 541 points?

Q32 When Charley Taylor caught 12 passes for touchdowns in 1966, he equaled a Redskin record. Who was the first Washington player to have 12 TD receptions?

WASHINGTON REDSKINS

A17   Sammy Baugh (November 3, 1940: 14 of 16 vs. the Steelers)

A18   Sammy Baugh (1945)

A19   Norm Snead (1963)

A20   Sonny Jurgensen (1967)

A21   Sonny Jurgensen (1964–74: 58.0)

A22   Jay Schroeder (1986: 4,109)

A23   Sammy Baugh (1945: 128 of 182, 70.3%)

A24   Charlie Gogolak (November 27, 1966: vs. Giants)

A25   Chris Hamburger (1966–69, 1972–76: nine. Ken Houston was in 10 Pro Bowls, but three came while he was with Houston.)

A26   Bobby Mitchell (1962: 72 points)
Jerry Smith (1967: 72 points)
George Rogers (1986: 108 points)

A27   91 games (from the 12th game in 1980 through the fifth game in 1986)

A28   Dick James (December 17, 1961: vs. Dallas)
Larry Brown (December 16, 1973: vs. Philadelphia)

A29   John Riggins (1983: 144)

A30   Charley Taylor (1964–77: 540)

A31   1983

A32   Hugh "Bones" Taylor

Q33   Art Monk's 106 catches in 1984 rewrote the NFL record books. Who was the previous holder of pro football's single-season reception mark, with 101 grabs?

Q34   Charley Taylor set a NFL record for receptions by a running back when he caught 53 passes in his rookie year (1964). Who broke Taylor's record?

Q35   Name the Redskin who holds the dubious distinction of catching the most passes in NFL history (201) without a touchdown.

Q36   Who holds the Washington single-game record for receiving yards, with 255?

Q37   There have been three pass completions of 99 yards in the history of the team. Name the combinations who linked up on these pass plays.

Q38   Two Redskins have caught 13 passes in one game. Name them.

Q39   Name the player who registered 269 receiving yards in a game against Washington.

Q40   Washington boasted of having both the winner and runner-up for the Rookie of the Year Award in 1964. Name this dynamic duo.

Q41   Who was the first Redskin to win NFL Rookie of the Year honors?

Q42   Who was the first free agent to rush for over 1,000 yards after the NFL-AFL 1970 merger?

Q43   Who was the first Redskin to capture the NFL rushing title?

Q44   Who was the first Redskin to crack the 1,000-yard rushing barrier?

Q45   Who were the first pair of Washington running backs to each gain 100 yards in the same game?

Q46   Who is Washington's career rushing leader?

Q47   Who set an NFL record with 45 rushing attempts in one game?

Q48   Two Redskins have more than 20 career 100-yard games. Name them.

Q49   Against what club did the Skins set a team record for rushing yards, with 352 in one game?

Q50   Which Skin holds the club record for rushing among QBs?

WASHINGTON REDSKINS

A33   Oiler Charley Hannigan (1964)

A34   Redskin Charley Harraway (1969: 55)

A35   Gerald Riggs

A36   Anthony Allen (October 4, 1987: vs. Cardinals; on seven receptions)

A37   October 15, 1939: Frank Filchock to Andy Farkas (vs. Pittsburgh)
September 15, 1963: George Izo to Bobby Mitchell (vs. Cleveland)
September 15, 1968: Sonny Jurgensen to Gerry Allen (vs. Chicago)

A38   Art Monk (November 4, 1990: vs. Detroit
               December 15, 1985: vs. Cincinnati)
Kelvin Bryant (December 7, 1986: vs. N.Y. Giants)

A39   Giant Del Shofner (October 28, 1962)

A40   Winner: Charley Taylor
Runner-up: Paul Krause

A41   Charley Taylor (1964)

A42   John Settle (1988: He was signed as a free agent by the Atlanta Falcons in 1987 and gained 1,024 yards in 1988.)

A43   Larry Brown (1970: 1,125 yards)

A44   Larry Brown (1970: 1,125 yards)

A45   George Rogers (104)
John Riggins (103)
(October 7, 1985: vs. St. Louis. The feat, which had taken Washington 49 years to accomplish, was matched four weeks later by Keith Griffin and Rogers, on November 3, 1985 against the Falcons.)

A46   John Riggins (7,472 yards)

A47   Jamie Morris (December 17, 1988: vs. Cincinnati)

A48   John Riggins (25)
Larry Brown (21)

A49   L.A. Rams (November 25, 1951)

A50   Joe Theismann

Q51 Who holds the highest average gain per rush over a career for the Redskins (minimum: 250 carries)?

Q52 The longest run from scrimmage for the Redskins is 88 yards. Who accomplished it?

Q53 What running back once gained 232 yards against the Skins—the most ever by an opponent?

Q54 Name the Washington player who holds the club record for the highest average gain per rush in a season (minimum: 100 carries).

Q55 Who holds the Skins' single-season rushing mark, with 1,347 yards?

Q56 Name the only three Redskin rushers to gain over 200 yards in a game.

Q57 John Riggins established an NFL record when he scored rushing TDs in 13 consecutive games from 1982 to 1983. Who ranks second with 12 straight games with a rushing TD?

Q58 Dexter Manley left the Redskins after the 1989 season as the club's all-time sack leader (97.5). Whose career club mark did Manley shatter?

Q59 The Redskins once registered 66 sacks in a season—a club record. In what year did they set the team mark?

Q60 Who was the first offensive lineman to score a touchdown for the Redskins?

Q61 John Riggins set an NFL record when he scored 24 TDs during the 1983 season. Whose single-season mark did he surpass?

Q62 Who set the club record for career TDs as a Redskin?

Q63 Who was the first NFL player to have three 2,000-yard seasons in net combined yards (rushing, receiving and returns)?

GLORY DAYS

Q1 What Redskin is the only NFL player to earn Super Bowl championship rings with three teams?

WASHINGTON REDSKINS

A51   Joe Theismann (1974–85: 5.1 yards per carry)

A52   Billy Wells (November 21, 1954: vs. St. Louis; it resulted in a TD.)

A53   Cleveland Brown Bobby Mitchell (November 15, 1959)

A54   Frank Atkins (1945: 5.42 yards per carry)

A55   John Riggins (1983)

A56   Gerald Riggs (September 17, 1989: 221 yards vs. Philadelphia)
George Rogers (December 21, 1985: 206 yards vs. St. Louis)
Timmy Smith (January 31, 1988: 204 yards vs. Denver in Super Bowl XXII)

A57   Redskin George Rogers (1985–86)

A58   Diron Talbert's (56)

A59   1984

A60   Joe Jacoby ("Jake the Quake" fell on a Keith Griffin fumble in the end zone in a November 29, 1984 game against the Vikings in Minneapolis.)

A61   O. J. Simpson's (23 TDs; Jerry Rice also scored 23 touchdowns in 1987.)

A62   Charley Taylor (90)

A63   Terry Metcalf

A1   Matt Millen (Oakland/L.A. Raiders—Super Bowls XV and XVIII
San Francisco 49ers—XXIV
Washington—XXVI)

GLORY DAYS

Q2   The Redskins have appeared in five Super Bowls. Name the only team to have reached the Super Bowl more times.

Q3   The Redskins routed the Giants 49–14 to become the 1937 Eastern champions. Who scored TDs of 75 yards and 76 yards on two rushing plays?

Q4   Despite freezing weather and a frozen field, Washington won the 1937 NFL title played at Soldier Field. Who was the Washington receiver who caught nine passes (160 yards), including 77-yard and 55-yard touchdowns?

Q5   The Skins took the worst drubbing in football history in the 1940 championship game when they lost 73-0 against Chicago. How many interceptions were thrown that day by Washington quarterbacks?

Q6   With only 55 seconds gone in the 1940 NFL title game, the Bears scored on a 68-yard end sweep. Whose romp was a sign of things to come in the contest?

Q7   Name the three Redskins who combined to throw eight interceptions in the 73–0 Bear rout in the 1940 NFL title game.

Q8   This Redskin not only made a critical interception during the 1942 championship game, but he also was on the receiving end of a 38-yard TD pass to lead Washington to a 14–6 win over Chicago. Name this two-way MVP.

Q9   The Redskins lost the 1943 NFL title 41–21, partly due to an early concussion suffered by Sammy Baugh. Who was Baugh attempting to tackle when his bell was rung?

Q10   Who replaced Sammy Baugh when the tailback suffered a concussion during the 1943 title game?

Q11   The 1945 NFL title was decided by a safety and resulted in a 15–14 Redskin loss. What were the unique circumstances surrounding the decisive play?

Q12   What Redskin intercepted two passes during the 1959 championship game, returning one of them 42 yards for a touchdown?

Q13   An early blocked punt resulted in a Washington score in the 1971 playoff game. Which Redskin gave the team its great field position?

WASHINGTON REDSKINS

A2   Dallas Cowboys (six)

A3   Cliff Battles

A4   Wayne Millner

A5   Eight

A6   Bill Osmanski

A7   Frank Filchock (4)
Sammy Baugh (2)
Roy Zimmerman (2)

A8   Wilbur Moore

A9   Sid Luckman

A10   George Cafego

A11   Sammy Baugh's pass from the end zone hit the goalpost, giving the Rams a safety. The rule is no longer in force.

A12   John Sample

A13   Jon Jaqua

*** FAST FACTS ***

Redskin head coach Curly Lambeau (1952–53) played varsity football at Notre Dame under Knute Rockne in 1918. He shared the Irish backfield with running back George Gipp before he withdrew from college in 1919.

The Washington Redskins are the only team in NFL history to win a world championship in their first year of existence. They accomplished it when the franchise moved from Boston in 1937. Later that season, the club defeated the Chicago Bears 28–21 for the NFL title.

In 1991, Mark Rypien became the first nontouring pro to participate in a golf tour event when he played in the Kemper Open at Avenel Country Club in Bethesda, Maryland.

Otto Graham made history when he was selected as a collegiate All-American in two sports in the same year. He was placed on both the basketball and football teams in 1943–44.

Q14 In the 1971 playoff game, Washington jumped to a 10–3 halftime lead, but couldn't hold on and eventually lost 24–20. Name the San Francisco players who combined on a 78-yard scoring pass to start the second half.

Q15 The Redskins were the 1972 Eastern Division champions in the NFC and defeated Green Bay in the first round of the playoffs that year. Who scored the only touchdown in the game in Washington's 16–3 victory?

Q16 Though Washington scored 26 points in the 1972 NFC title game, only two players accounted for all of the Redskin scoring. Who are they?

Q17 The only points scored by the Redskins in Super Bowl VII came on a blocked field goal try that was returned for a TD. Name the player who blocked the Miami kick and the teammate who ran it in for six points.

Q18 In the first quarter of Super Bowl VII, Bob Griese hit Howard Twilly for a 28-yard TD to put Miami on the scoreboard. Who did Twilly beat on the reception?

Q19 Name the Dolphin safety who was named the MVP of Super Bowl VII after he intercepted two Billy Kilmer passes.

Q20 Washington and Dallas had similar win-loss records at the end of the 1973 season, but the Cowboys were awarded the divisional title. What tie-breaker was used to give the Texas club the edge?

Q21 Though the club shared the best record in the NFC, the Skins were ousted early in the 1973 playoffs. Who ended Washington's hopes of back-to-back Super Bowl appearances with a 27–20 victory?

Q22 Though they were tied for the 1974 NFC Eastern Division title, the Redskins were demoted to wild-card status. What team took the division crown that year due to a pair of regular-season victories over Washington?

Q23 The score was 13–10 in the fourth quarter of the 1974 playoff game between Washington and L.A. when an interception resulted in a Ram TD. Who picked off Jurgensen's pass and killed the Redskins' hopes?

Q24 In the first round of the 1982 playoffs, Washington devastated Detroit, 31–7. Name the receiver who caught three touchdown passes to lead the Skins to victory.

Q25 The Redskins defeated their old nemesis, the Cowboys, to win the 1982 NFC Championship. On their way to a 31–17 victory, Washington knocked Dallas's starting QB, Danny White, out of the game in the first half. Who laid the hit on White?

WASHINGTON REDSKINS

A14   John Brodie to Gene Washington

A15   Jerry Smith (on a pass from Billy Kilmer)

A16   Charley Taylor (on two TD passes from Billy Kilmer)
Curt Knight (on a playoff-record four field goals and 2 PATs)
(The Redskins defeated Dallas, 26–3.)

A17   Bill Brundige blocked Garo Yepremian's attempt.
Mike Bass ran the ball in for a Redskin touchdown.

A18   Pat Fischer

A19   Jake Scott

A20   Point differential (In the two head-to-head meetings that season, Dallas was a + 13-point winner over Washington, even though the two clubs had split the series.)

A21   Minnesota Vikings

A22   St. Louis Cardinals

A23   Isiah Robertson (59-yard interception return for a TD)

A24   Alvin Garrett

A25   Dexter Manley

Q26　When John Riggins rushed for 166 yards in Super Bowl XVII, he set two postseason rushing records. What were they?

Q27　Of the 49 Redskins who participated in Super Bowl XVII, how many were free agent signees?

Q28　Name the Miami player who returned a Mark Moseley kickoff in the second quarter 98 yards for a Dolphin TD.

Q29　On a fourth-and-one situation in the fourth quarter of Super Bowl XVII, John Riggins broke free and scored on a 43-yard run. Whose tackle did he break to give Washington the lead?

Q30　The outcome of Super Bowl XVII was in doubt until Washington scored a TD with 1:55 left in the game. Who was on the receiving end of a Theismann six-yard scoring pass to clinch it for the Tribe?

Q31　Joe Theismann tied a Super Bowl record when he tossed eight consecutive complete passes during the 1982 classic. Whose mark did he equal?

Q32　In the 1982 NFL title game, John Riggins broke four Super Bowl game records previously held by Steeler Franco Harris. Name them.

Q33　Who was selected as the Most Valuable Player of Super Bowl XVII?

Q34　Which of these is NOT on the Super Bowl rings given to the Redskins for their victory in 1982?
(A) The Capitol Dome
(B) The score of the game
(C)The team motto ("Hail to the Redskins")
(D) Tampa Stadium
(E) Each player's name and number

Q35　Five minutes into Super Bowl XVIII, disaster struck for the Redskins. Who blocked a Jeff Hayes punt and recovered it in the end zone for a Raider TD?

Q36　There were only 12 seconds left in the first half of Super Bowl XVIII when Joe Thiesmann's sideline pass was intercepted deep in the Redskins' zone and returned it for five yards for a Raider touchdown. Who was on the receiving end of Theismann's errant throw?

Q37　Whose third-quarter 74-yard TD run broke the Redskins' back and essentially ended Super Bowl XVIII?

WASHINGTON REDSKINS

A26   Most yards in a Super Bowl game.
Four straight playoff games, with 100 yards rushing.

A27   26

A28   Fulton Walker

A29   Cornerback Don McNeal's

A30   Charlie Brown

A31   K.C.'s Len Dawson's (Super Bowl I)

A32   Most rushing attempts (Riggins: 38; Harris: 34)
Most rushing yards (Riggins: 166; Harris: 158)
Longest TD run from scrimmage (Riggins: 43; Harris: 22)
Most combined attempts (Riggins: 39; Harris 35)

A33   John Riggins

A34   (D)

A35   Derrick Jensen

A36   LB Jack Squirek

A37   Marcus Allen's

*** FAST FACT ***

Most Points, Both Teams: 113
Most PAT Attempts: 10 (Charlie Gogolak)
Most Points, One Team (Regular Season): 72
Most TDs, Both Teams: 16
Most Kickoff Returns, Both Teams: 19

Q38   Ricky Sanders set a new Super Bowl record with 193 receiving yards in the 1988 game against the Broncos. Whose mark did he surpass?

Q39   The Redskins were shocked to find themselves down by seven points with less than a minute gone in Super Bowl XXII. Who was the passing combination that hooked up for a 56-yard TD on the first play of the game?

Q40   The Skins set an NFL record when they scored 35 points in the second quarter of Super Bowl XXII. How many TD passes did Doug Williams toss in that period?

Q41   Timmy Smith broke the Super Bowl rushing mark when he gained 204 yards in the 1988 NFL title game. Who held the record prior to Smith's performance?

Q42   Ricky Sanders set a new Super Bowl record when he totaled 193 receiving yards in the 1988 NFL title game. Who held the old record of 161 yards?

Q43   Who has since broken Sanders's mark?

Q44   Who was the MVP of Super Bowl XXII?

Q45   With the Vikings driving to score the tying TD in the 1989 NFC title game, the Redskins recovered a Darrin Nelson fumble to stem the comeback. Who forced the Minnesota turnover on the Washington goal line?

Q46   In the 1992 divisional playoff game, the Redskins routed the Falcons by a score of 24–7. Who scored the only TD for Atlanta?

Q47   The tone was set in the 1982 NFC title contest when Lion QB Erik Kramer was sacked on the first play of the game, causing a fumble that the Skins recovered. Who caused the sack and who recovered the loose ball for Washington?

Q48   Whose 32-yard interception return for a TD ended the scoring for Washington in its 41–10 1992 NFC Championship defeat of the Detroit Lions?

Q49   Much was made of the Washington players who went ice-fishing in the days prior to Super Bowl XXVI in Minneapolis. Name the quartet of Redskins who went fishing.

Q50   The start of the second half in Super Bowl XXVI resulted in a backbreaking blow for the Bills when QB Jim Kelly was hurried into throwing an interception. Who rushed the Buffalo and who nabbed it?

WASHINGTON REDSKINS

A38   Lynn Swann's

A39   John Elway to Ricky Nattiel

A40   Four (80 yards to Sanders
               27 yards to Clark
               50 yards to Sanders
               8 yard pass to Didier)

A41   Raider Marcus Allen (Super Bowl XVIII: 191 yards)

A42   Pittsburgh's Lynn Swann

A43   Jerry Rice (Super Bowl XXIII: 215 yards)

A44   Doug Williams

A45   Darrell Green

A46   Tracy Johnson

A47   Charles Mann sacked Kramer.
Fred Stokes recovered the loose ball.

A48   Darrell Green

A49   Art Monk
Chip Lohmiller
Monte Coleman
Earnest Byner

A50   Andre Collins was in Kelly's face.
Kurt Gouveia caught the pass intended for Thurman Thomas.

Q51   Whose fourth-quarter 60-yard interception in Super Bowl XXVI was returned for a touchdown and ended the scoring for Washington?

Q52   Mark Rypien was selected as the Super Bowl XXVI MVP. Who was the runner-up for the award?

Q53   Joe Theismann is the only quarterback to win the Super Bowl while wearing Number 7. Which number is the most popular among victorious QBs?

TRADES, WAIVES, AND ACQUISITIONS

Q1   Who is the first Heisman Trophy winner to be drafted by the Redskins?

Q2   Name the placekicker who was the first at his position to be selected as a team's number one choice in the draft.

Q3   Who was the first player ever drafted by the Washington Redskins?

Q4   Who came to the U.S. capital when Jimmy Johnston was traded to the Chicago Cardinals in 1941?

Q5   The Redskins were persistent when they selected the same player twice, using first-round draft choices in 1945 and 1946, but they failed to lure the collegian to D.C. Who snubbed the Tribe?

Q6   Receiver Steve Bagarus was dealt to the Rams in a 1947 trade that brought two new players to Washington. Name the acquisitions.

Q7   In 1947, Turk Edwards read in a magazine about an Oklahoma City University end who caught nine TDs in 41 minutes' playing time the previous year, so he went out and signed him up as a free agent. Name the receiver who would spend eight years on the Skins' roster due to that article.

Q8   The Redskins traded for "Bullet Bill" Dudley from Detroit in 1949. Who did they give up for him?

Q9   The Skins' 1949 first-round pick was also selected in the first round of the previous year's draft by Chicago, but NFL Commissioner Bert Bell ruled the Bears' selection invalid because the collegian was then only a junior. Name the two-time first-round pick.

WASHINGTON REDSKINS

A51   Alvin Walton's

A52   Brad Edwards

A53   Number 12 (10 winners)

A1   Desmond Howard (1992)

A2   Charlie Gogolak (1965)

A3   Andy Farkus (Farkus was selected in the first round of the 1938 draft. The club moved from Boston after the 1937 season, making the 1938 pick Washington's first.)

A4   Ki Aldrich

A5   Cal Rossi (UCLA)

A6   Ralph Ruthstrom
Tom Farmer

A7   Hugh Taylor

A8   Dan Sandifer

A9   Texas A & M's Rob Goode

TRADES, WAIVES, AND ACQUISITIONS

Q10   Five times during the 1950s, the Skins used their number one pick in the draft to select a quarterback. Who were the signal callers chosen?

Q11   Name the University of Kentucky product who was Washington's first-round pick in the 1954 draft?

Q12   In a two-for-one trade, the Redskins obtained Johnny Carson and Dale Atkeson from Cleveland in a 1954 deal. Who did they give up?

Q13   Dick Modzelewski was traded to Pittsburgh in 1955. Name the two Steelers who came to D.C.

Q14   Bert Zagers was acquired from the Lions in 1957 for what Redskin QB?

Q15   Name the two players traded to Detroit in 1955 so that Washington could have the services of linebacker Torgy Torgeson.

Q16   The Skins' used their number one pick in the 1956 draft to select a University of Maryland running back, but the local star opted to play four seasons in the Canadian Football League before signing with Washington in 1960. Name him.

Q17   The Skins' 1957 first-round choice was a fullback out of the University of Miami. Name this All-American.

Q18   Who did the Redskins trade in order to acquire fullback John "Johnny Oh" Olszewski from the Chicago Cardinals in 1958?

Q19   Washington used the Eagles' number three pick in the 1958 draft to select end Bill Anderson. Who did they have to trade to Philly for the choice?

Q20   Quarterback George Izo became a Redskin on September 12, 1961, through a trade with the Cardinals. Who did Washington send to St. Louis in the transaction?

Q21   Who came to Washington when the club traded offensive end/fullback John Olszewski to Detroit in 1961?

Q22   The Redskins sent Cleveland the number one pick in the 1962 draft for two players. Who came to the capital in return?

Q23   In 1961, the Skins made a four-for-two deal with the Giants that landed them Jerry Daniels, Fred Dugan, John Aveni, and Gene Cronin. What players did Washington sacrifice in the trade?

WASHINGTON REDSKINS

A10   Larry Isbell (1951)
Jack Scarbath(1952)
Ralph Guglielmi (1954)
Don Allard (1958)
Richie Lucas (1959)

A11   Steve Meilinger

A12   Halfback Don Paul

A13   Art DeCarlo
Leo Elter

A14   Harry Gilmer

A15   Jim Ricca
Walt Yowarsky

A16   Ed Vereb

A17   Don Bosseler

A18   Tackle Ben Preston

A19   Al Dorow

A20   QB Ralph Guglielmi

A21   Steve Junker

A22   Bobby Mitchell
LeRoy Jackson
(The Browns used the pick to select All-American Ernie Davis. Davis died
before he played in the NFL.)

A23   Jim Podoley
Joe Walton

TRADES, WAIVES, AND ACQUISITIONS

Q24 The Redskins sent the Bears their number one pick in the 1965 draft for two of Chicago's players. Name the pair who came from the Windy City to the Capital City.

Q25 Sonny Jurgensen came to Washington on April 1, 1964, through a trade with Philadelphia. Who did the Skins have to give up for the future Hall of Famer?

Q26 Nine days after Sonny Jurgensen was acquired, the Redskins continued their changing ways. Sam Huff and rookie George Seals came from the Giants for two players and a draft pick. Who did Washington give up in that trade?

Q27 Who came to D.C. when All-Pro safety Paul Krause was traded to Minnesota?

Q28 Washington acquired Gary Beban from Los Angeles in 1968 before the Rams' second-round pick ever played a down in the NFL. What did the Redskins give up for the quarterback?

Q29 The Skins sent Lonnie Sanders off to St. Louis in 1968. Who did the club acquire in exchange for the defensive halfback?

Q30 The Redskins sent All-Pro safety Paul Krause to the Vikings in 1968 for a 1969 draft pick and a tight end. Name the player who Washington picked up.

Q31 A University of Maryland tackle, the Skins acquired him from the Rams in 1968 for their first-round pick in the 1970 draft, and he would play six seasons with the club. Name him.

Q32 The Redskins' first pick in the 1970 draft was a second-round selection from the University of Colorado. Name the defensive tackle chosen by Washington.

Q33 Washington sent running back Henry Dyer to Cincinnati in a 1971 trade. Name the quarterback who came to the Redskins in the exchange.

Q34 The Skins beat the deadline when they acquired receiver Clifton McNeil through a trade on October 26, 1971, the final day for trades that season. Who did Washington give up in the deal with the Giants?

Q35 George Allen's "future is now" philosophy took hold quickly as Washington went to the playoffs in the first four years that he coached the Redskins. What was the club's highest pick in the draft from the years 1972 to 1979?

WASHINGTON REDSKINS

A24   Fred Williams
Angelo Coia

A25   Norm Snead
Claude Crabb

A26   Andy Stynchula
Dick James

A27   Marlin McKeever

A28   Their first-round pick in the 1969 draft

A29   DB Jim Burson

A30   Marlin McKeever

A31   Walter Rock

A32   Bill Brundige

A33   Sam Wyche

A34   Richmond Flowers

A35   Fourth round (1977 and 1979; in 1972, the club did not have a selection until the eighth round.)

*** FAST FACTS ***

The "Fun Bunch" had more of an effect on the NFL than they expected. The group of seven Redskins would celebrate TDs by gathering in the end zone and exchanging high fives while leaping into the air. Partly as a result, the league banned choreographed celebrations because it was felt that it was demeaning to competing teams.

RECORDS SET IN REDSKINS' 72–41 DEFEAT OF GIANTS— NOVEMBER 27, 1966

In 18 NFL seasons (1957–63, Eagles; 1964–74, Redskins), Sonny Jurgensen played on only eight teams that had records better than .500.

During the 1987 players' strike, the Washington Redskins were the only players to remain unified throughout the walkout. No regulars returned to the field during the entire length of the four-week labor battle.

TRADES, WAIVES, AND ACQUISITIONS

Q36 George Allen traded away the Skins' first-round draft choice in the 1972 draft to the New York Jets. What player was acquired for the pick?

Q37 The Redskins' first-round pick in the 1973 draft was sent to Baltimore along with Cotton Speyrer for what Colt wide receiver?

Q38 Linebacker Brad Dusek was traded to Washington in 1973 from New England. What Redskin became a Patriot?

Q39 The acquisition of safety Ken Houston from the Oilers in 1973 cost the Redskins five players. Name the quintet shipped off to the Lone Star State.

Q40 Dave Butz did not come cheaply to the Redskins when the team signed the free agent in 1975. What did Washington send to St. Louis for the All-Pro defensive tackle?

Q41 Joe Lavender was acquired by the Skins in a 1976 trade with the Eagles. Who did the club give up for the defensive back?

Q42 The Redskins drafted two placekickers during the 1980s. Who were they?

Q43 Jeris White came to Washington from Tampa Bay in a 1980 trade. Who did the Skins give up in the deal?

Q44 Name the two quarterbacks who were swapped in a 1982 trade between the Skins and the Patriots.

Q45 Darrell Green was selected by Washington in the first round of the 1983 draft. Who was the next first-round pick by the Skins?

Q46 From what team did Washington acquire the rights to Ricky Sanders in a 1986 trade?

Q47 The Skins sent Charlie Brown packing to Atlanta in a 1985 preseason trade. What Falcon came to Washington in the exchange?

Q48 Who did the Redskins trade to the Raiders in 1988 for All-Pro tackle Jim Lachey?

Q49 Earnest Byner was acquired in a April 22, 1989, trade with Cleveland. Who did Washington send to the Browns for the running back?

Q50 Eric Williams was picked up from the Lions in a September 1990 trade. Who did the Skins give up in the deal?

WASHINGTON REDSKINS

A36 Defensive end Verlon Biggs

A37 Roy Jefferson

A38 Donnell Smith

A39 Mack Alston
Jim Snowden
Jeff Severson
Clifton McNeil
Mike Fanucci

A40 The first-round draft picks and a second-round pick (At the time, it was the largest compensation deal in NFL history.)

A41 Manny Sistrunk

A42 Danny Miller (1982: 11th round)
Chip Lohmiller (1988: second round)

A43 Danny Buggs

A44 Tom Flick went to New England.
Tow Owen came to Washington.

A45 Bobby Wilson (1991)

A46 New England Patriots

A47 RC Thielemann

A48 Jay Schroeder

A49 Mike Oliphant

A50 James Wilder (plus a 1991 fourth-round draft choice)

Baltimore Colts

BALTIMORE COLTS

1983 BALTIMORE COLTS

Row 1 (left to right) John Lopez, Head Trainer; Hunter Smith, Assistant Trainer; Raul Allegre, Rohn Stark, Mark Reed, Mark Herrmann, Jim Bob Taylor, Mike Pagel, Alvin Moore, Nesby Glasgow, Kim Anderson, Cleveland Franklin, Mark Kafentzis, Larry Anderson, Zachary Dixon, Jon Scott, Equipment Manager; Bradley Rogers, Assistant Equipment Manager **Row 2** Coach Gunther Cunningham, Randy McMillian, Curtis Dickey, Jeff Delaney, Newton Williams, Derrick Hatchett, Kendall Williams, James Burroughs, Marco Tongue, Cliff Odom, Grant Feasel, Ricky Jones, Greg Bracelin, Ray Donaldson, Sanders Shiver, Coach Zeke Bratkowski **Row 3** General Manager Ernie Accorsi; Head Coach Frank Kush, Barry Krauss, Vernon Maxwell, Mike Humiston, Gary Padjen, Ben Utt, Jeff Hart, Leo Wisniewski, Karl Baldischwiler, Steve Wright, Sid Abramowitz, Chris Hinton, Jim Mills, Steve Parker, Coach Hal Hunter; Coach Richard Mann, Jim Irsay, Player Personnel **Row 4** Coach Bob Valesente; Coach Roger Theder, Raymond Butler, Pat Beach, Tim Sherwin, Victor Oatis, Matt Bouza, Phil Smith, Tracy Porter, Bernard Henry, Hosea Taylor, Quinton Ballard, Ernie Barnes, Johnie Cooks, Donnell Thompson; Coach Rick Venturi; Coach Mike Westhoff

THE SUITS

Q1   Name the 10 men who coached the Colts in the team's 31-year run in Baltimore (1953–83).

Q2   Which Colt coach was a member of the Dallas Texans when the team was awarded to Baltimore in early 1953?

Q3   Which Colt pilot received several Coach of the Year accolades when he raised the team from a 2–12 record in 1974 to the 1975 AFC Eastern Division title and a 10–4 mark?

Q4   Who was the Colts' head coach in 1953, the year pro football reappeared in Baltimore?

Q5   Weeb Ewbank was fired after the 1962 season. What was the club's record that year?

Q6   What feat did Weeb Ewbank accomplish as a coach that can never be duplicated?

Q7   What is Weeb Ewbank's given name?

Q8   Weeb Ewbank and Paul Brown were teammates at Miami (Ohio) University, and later they coached together for two different teams. Where did the two hook up?

Q9   What sport did Weeb Ewbank coach for 13 years at Miami?

Q10   In 1960, Don Shula took his first NFL coaching job. With what team was Shula a defensive coach?

Q11   With what skipper did Don Shula share Coach of the Year honors in 1967?

BALTIMORE COLTS

A1   Keith Molesworth (1953)   Howard Schneellenberger (1973–74)
         Weeb Ewbank (1954–62)   Joe Thomas (1974)
         Don Shula (1963–69)   Ted Marchibroda (1975–79)
         Don McCafferty (1970–72)   Mike McCormack (1980–81)
         John Sandusky (1972)   Frank Kush (1982–83)

A2   Mike McCormack

A3   Ted Marchibroda

A4   Keith Molesworth (3–9)

A5   7–7

A6   He won championships in both the National and American Football
         League.

A7   Wilbur

A8   Great Lakes Naval Station (during World War II)
         Cleveland Browns (Ewbank was Brown's tackle coach from 1949 to 53.)

A9   Basketball

A10   Detroit Lions

A11   George Allen of the Rams

*** FAST FACTS ***

Top Five Guns in Colt History	Passing Yards
Johnny Unitas	39,768
Bert Jones	17,663
Earl Morrall	5,666
Mike Pagel	3,634
Marty Domres	3,471

Super Bowl V was the first NFL title game to be played under the new
merger arrangement between the NFL and AFL.

Don "The Bowling Ball" Nottingham was taken by the Colts in the 17th
round of the 1971 draft. He was the 341st pick out of 342 players
selected.

THE SUITS

Q12   Don McCafferty's easygoing style led to a nickname being pinned on the Colt coach. What did his players call him?

Q13   Known as the tallest coach in the NFL (6'5"), Don McCafferty was named skipper of the team in 1970. How long had he worked as an assistant Colt coach before he was elevated to the top spot?

Q14   Under what two legendary coaches did Howard Schnellenberger work as an assistant before he took the reins of the Hosses in 1973?

Q15   A quarterback at St. Bonaventure and the University of Detroit, Ted Marchibroda was this NFL club's first-round pick in 1953. What team showed that confidence in Marchibroda?

Q16   With what team was Mike McCormack toiling as the offensive line coach before he took the Colt helm in 1980?

Q17   During his 22-year tenure as head coach at Arizona State, Frank Kush racked up an impressive .764 winning percentage. Whom did Kush succeed in the top job at Arizona in 1958?

Q18   With what Canadian Football League franchise did Frank Kush break into the pro coaching ranks?

THE UNIFORMS

Q1   Who was the first player from the Colts to reach the hallowed halls of the Pro Football Hall of Fame?

Q2   The first man to be elected to the NFL Hall of Fame who was solely an offensive lineman was a Colt. Name this Baltimore product.

Q3   Who was the onetime Colt who added a new word to the football vocabulary—sack"?

Q4   Which Colt Hall of Famer was born in Guatemala City, Guatemala?

Q5   Considered one of the toughest men to defense in the league, this All-American back stood just 5'4" tall. Who was he?

BALTIMORE COLTS

A12   "The Easy Rider"

A13   11 years

A14   George Allen—Los Angeles
Don Shula—Miami

A15   Pittsburgh Steelers

A16   Cincinnati Bengals

A17   Dan Devine

A18   Hamilton Tiger-Cats (in 1981)

A1   Art Donovan (1968)

A2   Jim Parker

A3   Deacon Jones (Deacon called the play a sack because "you need a short term that can fit easily into the newspaper headlines.")

A4   Ted Hendricks

A5   Buddy Young

Q6 The Colts were the first team in league history with successive Rookie of the Year winners. Which outstanding first-year players were so honored?

Q7 Identify this Colt duo: They came off the same Boston College team, both were linemen, they had the same first name, and both joined the Colts in 1950.

Q8 The Colts opened the 1953 season with a 13–9 upset of the Chicago Bears. Name the kicker who nailed a 56-yard field goal in the Colts' debut.

Q9 What team made Gino Marchetti its number one pick in the 1952 draft?

Q10 Gino Marchetti played in every Pro Bowl from 1954 to '64, with the exception of the 1958 game. Why did he miss the contest that year?

Q11 Gino Marchetti called it quits after the 1964 season, but in response to an emergency call from the Colts, he returned to the team in 1966. How many games did he play during that campaign?

Q12 Alan Ameche had an unusual job in the off-season. How did the Horse supplement his income?

Q13 This early-day Colt back survived the Texas City, Texas, explosion of 1947 that killed 650 people. Who was the man known as "Long Gone"?

Q14 Of the 631 times that Raymond Berry handled the ball in his NFL career, how many times did he fumble?

Q15 From what college did Johnny Unitas graduate?

Q16 What club drafted Johnny Unitas with a 1955 ninth-round draft pick, only to cut him before he'd thrown a single pass in a preseason game?

Q17 For what team was Johnny Unitas playing when the Colts signed him as a free agent in 1956?

Q18 Four games into the 1956 season, Johnny Unitas got his opportunity to play when the Colts' starting QB was injured. Whose misfortune gave Unitas the chance he needed?

Q19 Johnny Unitas's first pass in his first NFL game resulted in an interception. Who was the Chicago Bear on the receiving end of the Hall of Famer's inaugural toss?

Q20 Johnny Unitas copped the NFL's Most Valuable Player Award in 1967, but because of injury, he was unable to vie for the distinction the following year. Who captured the MVP honor in 1968?

BALTIMORE COLTS

A6   Alan Ameche (1955)
          Lenny Moore (1956)

A7   Art Donovan
          Art Spinney

A8   Bert Rechichar

A9   New York Yanks

A10   He missed the game because he suffered a broken ankle in the "sudden death" championship game against the Giants.

A11   Four

A12   He was a pro wrestling referee.

A13   L. G. Dupre

A14   One

A15   University of Louisville

A16   Pittsburgh Steelers

A17   Bloomfield Rams (semipro team)

A18   George Shaw

A19   J. C. Caroline (The Colts lost the game 58–27.)

A20   His teammate, Earl Morrall (Morrall also won the NFL passing crown that season.)

Q21   To whom did John Unitas throw the last pass of his brilliant career with the Colts?

Q22   In what year was Johnny Unitas traded from the Colts?

Q23   With what club did Johnny Unitas finish his NFL career?

Q24   How many times did Johnny Unitas lead the NFL in interceptions?

Q25   This Colt played linebacker at Ohio State, started at guard and tackle in the pros, and snared the Outland Trophy in 1956. Name this outstanding athlete.

Q26   In what two Halls of Fame is Jim Parker an inductee?

Q27   Which Colt running back was discovered by a San Francisco 49er scout while he was playing service football in the navy?

Q28   What team did "Instant Quarterback" Tom Matte help beat when he stepped in at QB in a 1965 game that tied the Colts for first place with the Packers?

Q29   John Mackey, who served as president of the NFL Players Association, was accorded an honor during the 50th anniversary of the league. How was he feted?

Q30   What two positions did Lou Michaels play in his career with the Colts?

Q31   Name the book written by Colt linebacker Mike Curtis.

Q32   This Colt standout led Michigan State to two consecutive undefeated seasons and was a force in the legendary 10–10 tie with Notre Dame in 1966. Name him.

Q33   Ted Hendricks appeared in 215 consecutive games during his pro career. Name the clubs he played for over that span.

Q34   Which Colt back shattered O. J. Simpson's NCAA record for rushing yardage in a season with 1,720 in 1970?

Q35   At what school did Don Cunningham put his name in the record books after he became the school's all-time rusher with 2,515 yards?

Q36   Ray May once portrayed a teammate in this descriptive fashion: "You have to hit him very, very low—like around the neck." To whom was May referring?

BALTIMORE COLTS

A21 Johnny U's final toss was a touchdown to Eddie Hinton on December 3, 1972.

A22 1973 (January 22)

A23 San Diego Chargers

A24 Twice (1961: 24
              1966: 24)

A25 Jim Parker

A26 Pro Football Hall of Fame
National Football Foundation Hall of Fame

A27 Joe Perry. His only college ball experience was at Compton, (California) Junior College.

A28 Los Angeles Rams (20–17; with Matte at the controls, the Colts lost to the Packers in the playoffs.)

A29 He was voted the greatest tight end to play pro football.

A30 Placekicker
Defensive end

A31 *Keep Off of My Turf*

A32 Bubba Smith

A33 Baltimore Colts
Green Bay Packers
Oakland Raiders
L.A. Raiders

A34 Don McCauley

A35 Kent State

A36 Don Nottingham

Q21. To whom did Johnny Unitas throw the last pass of his brilliant career with the Colts?

BALTIMORE COLTS

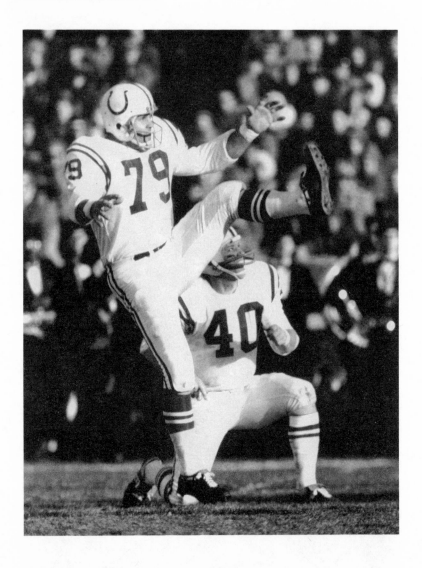

Q18. What sixties era Colt kicker set a club mark when he nailed 103 consecutive PATs?

Q37 Originally the Chargers' number one selection in the 1969 draft, this QB was dispatched to the Colts three years later for John Andrews and a draftee. Name the signal caller who joined the Hosses on October 7, 1972.

Q38 For what team was Dub Jones, Bert's father, a star receiver?

Q39 Bert Jones was selected with the second overall pick in the 1973 draft. Who was taken ahead of the LSU quarterback?

Q40 The Colts used the Saints' choice to select Bert Jones in the first round of the 1973 draft. What did Baltimore have to send to the Bayou for the selection?

Q41 Which versatile Colt was an accomplished sculptor and tree surgeon in the off-season?

Q42 Deacon Jones began his career with the Rams and finished it with the Colts. With what other club did he play in the NFL?

Q43 Deacon Jones played 14 seasons in the NFL. How many games did he miss due to injury?

Q44 Which Colt kicker was born in Donawitz, Austria, where he was named to several all-star soccer teams?

Q45 Identify the Colt who was plucked by the Falcons in the first round of the 1969 draft and was the second player chosen behind O. J. Simpson.

Q46 True or false—Greg Landry was the first quarterback selected in the 1968 draft.

Q47 Identify the Colt quarterback who joined his wife as inductees of the Massachusetts Hall of Fame.

Q48 Newcomers Alan Ameche (1955) and Norm Bulaich (1970) paved the way for other Colt rookies when each man led his team in rushing. Who was the third freshman back to top the team in rushing?

Q49 What do Tim Berry and Marvin Sims have in common?

Q50 Who were the trio of players selected ahead of Art Schlichter in the 1982 draft?

Q51 Who started at quarterback for the Colts in 1982, the strike-shortened season during which each team played a total of nine games?

BALTIMORE COLTS

A37   Marty Domres

A38   Cleveland Browns

A39   John Matuszak (by the Houston Oilers)

A40   Defensive tackle Billy Newsome and the Colts' fourth-round selection (Stanford's Jim Merlo was selected by New Orleans with the pick.)

A41   Mike Barnes

A42   San Diego Chargers (1972–73)

A43   Three

A44   Toni Linhart

A45   George Kunz

A46   True (by Detroit)

A47   Greg Landry (whose wife, Jeannine, was an outstanding gymnast)

A48   Curtis Dickey (1980)

A49   Both players made the team after being selected in the final round of their respective drafts. (Berry—1974; Sims—1980)

A50   Kenneth Sims (New England)
Johnnie Cooks (Baltimore)
Chip Banks (Cleveland)

A51   Mike Pagel

THE UNIFORMS

Q52 Recruited to Arizona State, this player was the first QB to pass for over 2,000 yards in consecutive seasons (1980 and 1981.) Identify the field general.

Q53 In what two sports did Rohn Stark earn All-American honors at Florida State?

Q54 When Rohn Stark was chosen in the second round of the 1982 draft, it marked the first time a punter was tabbed that high in the draft since New Orleans made a punter the top pick of the '79 draft. Who did the Saints select in the first round?

Q55 Who led the Colts in scoring in 1983, the team's last season in Baltimore?

Q56 What was distinctive about Chris Hinton's appearance in the 1983 Pro Bowl?

Q57 Which Colt had an impressive debut in the NFL when he won numerous awards, including 1983's Defensive Rookie of the Year Award?

Q58 Who was the last Baltimore-based Colt to appear in the Pro Bowl?

FYI

Q1 Baltimore was awarded an All-American Football Conference franchise in 1947 because a team had folded due to financial problems in the previous season. What city's failure began the Colts' distinguished history?

Q2 What place does Charles Evans hold in Colt history?

Q3 What were the original colors of the Colts in the All-American Football Conference?

Q4 How did the Colts acquire their blue and white team colors?

Q5 After the completion of the Colts' first NFL season, the team found itself fifth in the standings. Which four teams finished ahead of Baltimore, and which club was in the cellar of the Western Conference?

Q6 How long did it take the Colts before they were first in the Western Conference standings?

BALTIMORE COLTS

A52   Mike Pagel

A53   Football
Track

A54   Russell Erxleben

A55   Raul Allegre (112 points)

A56   Hinton was the first rookie starter on the AFC Pro Bowl offensive line since the 1970 AFL-NFL merger.

A57   Vernon Maxwell

A58   Chris Hinton (1983)

A1   Miami (The franchise was called the Seahawks.)

A2   The Middle River, Maryland, native was the winner in a 1947 contest to name the Baltimore franchise. (His "Colts" submission was selected out of 1,877 entries.)

A3   Green and silver

A4   Blue and white were the official colors of the Dallas Texans, the team that relocated to Baltimore in 1953.

A5   Detroit, San Francisco, Los Angeles, and Chicago all finished ahead of the Colts; Green Bay brought up the rear.

A6   In 1958, the Colts finished in first place with a 9–3 mark.

Q7   On May 10, 1969, the Colts, as part of the NFL's realignment, were switched to the American Conference. Which two teams joined the Hosses in the move?

Q8   What was the Colts' record in 1982, the year the players went on strike?

Q9   What was the Colts' win-loss record in 1983, their farewell season in Baltimore?

SETTING THE STANDARD

Q1   Identify the Colt who set a franchise record when he galloped 87 yards after he picked off a Bart Starr pass in a late 1965 game against the Packers.

Q2   Which Colt set a record in 1953, the year the team returned to Baltimore, by making 11 interceptions during that campaign?

Q3   Johnny Unitas holds eight of the top 10 passing-yardage records in franchise history. His best passing game came on September 17, 1967, when he was 22 or 32 for 401 yards. Against what team did Johnny U set a record for the ages?

Q4   Which dynamic duo hooked up for the team's longest pass completion ever when they connected for 90 yards in a 1975 game with the Jets?

Q5   Bert Jones set a team standard when he attempted 53 passes in a December 1974 contest versus the Jets. How many completions did Jones have on that pacesetting day?

Q6   On September 18, 1983, the Colts established a club record for penalty yards (153). Against what team did the Colts mark their version of Flag Day?

Q7   True or False—the Colts once played without being penalized.

Q8   In 1964, this Colt set a scoring record with 20 touchdowns and 120 points. Who set the franchise mark that has stood the test of time?

Q9   Name the only quarterback who is among the top 10 rushers in Colt history.

BALTIMORE COLTS

A7   Cleveland Browns
Pittsburgh Steelers

A8   0–8–1

A9   7–9

A1   Dave Robinson

A2   Tom Keane (none returned for touchdowns)

A3   Atlanta Falcons

A4   Bert Jones
Roger Carr

A5   36

A6   Buffalo Bills

A7   True (against Green Bay, at Milwaukee, on September 10, 1966)

A8   Lenny Moore

A9   Johnny Unitas (No. 9; 1,777 yards)

*** FAST FACTS ***

The 1983 edition of the Colts was the youngest in the NFL; the team averaged 24.2 years of age and 1.6 years of NFL experience. A dozen first-year men were on the roster.

Keith Molesworth and Don Kellett, the Colts' first coach and general manager, had been baseball teammates at second base and shortstop when they played briefly at Syracuse in the International League.

SETTING THE STANDARD

Q10   On September 25, 1955, Alan Ameche ran like a horse when he compiled 194 yards in a battle with the Bears. It took 16 years before Ameche's record was shattered by four yards. Who etched his name in the record books with a 198-yard rushing performance against the Jets?

Q11   Which Colt was the team's first 1,000-yard rusher?

Q12   Lydell Mitchell went down in team history as the player who ran for the most yards during the team's stay in Baltimore. How many yards did Mitchell chalk up during his milestone season of 1976?

Q13   Joe Washington is at the top of the Colts' single-game pass-reception list with 13 catches and 130 yards in a 1979 contest against the Chiefs. What other Baltimore player once racked up 13 receptions?

Q14   It took 25 years before a Colt rookie came anywhere near Alan Ameche's rookie rushing numbers. The Horse chalked up 961 yards in 1955. Which Colt first-year man ran for 800 yards in 1980?

Q15   Which Colt punter boomed a kick 76 yards against the New York Giants on October 17, 1971?

Q16   This Colt punter won the league championship in 1969 with a 45.3 average?

Q17   Who set a Colt standard with 50 kickoff returns and 1,126 yards during the 1979 season?

Q18   What sixties-era Colt kicker set a club mark when he nailed 103 consecutive PATs?

Q19   On November 13, 1983, the Colts set a team attendance record with their largest home crowd—61,479. What club were the Colts battling on that trendsetting day?

GLORY DAYS

Q1   The 1958 NFL Championship was the first sudden-death overtime game in league history. Who were the opposing head coaches?

Q2   What Colt broke his leg with less than three minutes left in the 1958 NFL title game and New York holding a 17–14 lead?

BALTIMORE COLTS

A10 Norm Bulaich (September 19, 1971)

A11 Lydell Mitchell (1,193 in 1975)

A12 1,200

A13 Lydell Mitchell (82 yards against the Jets; December 15, 1974)

A14 Curtis Dickey

A15 David Lee

A16 David Lee (His longest that season was 66 yards.)

A17 Nesby Glasgow

A18 Lou Michaels (1964–66)

A19 Pittsburgh Steelers

A1 Baltimore: Weeb Ewbank
New York: Jim Lee Howell

A2 Gino Marchetti (when his teammate Gene "Big Daddy" Lipscomb fell on him as he was tackling Frank Gifford)

Q3 With seven seconds left in regulation in the 1958 NFL Championship game, Baltimore booted the tying field goal from 13 yards out. Who was the kicker on the play?

Q4 New York won the toss and took the kickoff in the overtime period of the 1958 title game. Who caught the kickoff and returned it to the Giants' 20-yard line?

Q5 The final score of the 1958 title contest was 23–17 as the Colts scored on a one-yard run after 8:15 of overtime had elapsed. Who carried the ball on the winning rush?

Q6 To what team did the Colts fall victim in the 1965 sudden-death playoff game that determined the Western Conference champion?

Q7 Before the Colts snared the NFL Championship in 1966, they racked up more wins in a single season than any other club had been able to muster. How many victories did the club string together?

Q8 Under coach Don Shula, the Colts made their first Super Bowl appearance in 1968. In what division did the Hosses finish first with a 13–1 mark?

Q9 The Colts defeated the Vikings to earn their way to the 1968 NFL Championship game, but the Browns were a surprise winner in their match. Who did Cleveland defeat to get to the title game?

Q10 Who blocked a Cleveland field goal attempt in the first period of the 1968 NFL title contest?

Q11 Who scored three TDs in the 1968 NFL Championship game to lead the Colts to a 34–0 victory?

Q12 In the second quarter of Super Bowl III, the Colts tried a flea-flicker play that worked but resulted in an interception when Earl Morrall couldn't spot the receiver in the end zone. Name the end who was so open that he was frantically jumping up and down while waving his hands.

Q13 Who was the only Colt to score a touchdown in Super Bowl III?

Q14 What Colt running back rushed for 16 yards in Super Bowl III?

Q15 Two rookie coaches led their teams to Super Bowl wins. One was Don McCafferty. Who was the other?

Q16 At what stadium was Super Bowl V played?

BALTIMORE COLTS

A3   Steve Myhra

A4   Don Maynard

A5   Alan Ameche

A6   Green Bay Packers

A7   15

A8   Coastal Division

A9   Dallas Cowboys

A10   Bubba Smith blocked the 41-yard field goal attempt.

A11   Tom Matte

A12   Jimmy Orr (Morrall ended up throwing the ball to Jet defender Jim Hudson.)

A13   Jerry Hill (a one-yard carry with 3:19 left)

A14   Tom Matte

A15   George Seifert (Super Bowl XXIV; McCafferty did it in Super Bowl V.)

A16   The Orange Bowl in Miami

*** FAST FACTS ***

A six-week drive that saw Baltimore fans raise $300,000 in cash and the team sell 15,000 season tickets was the impetus behind the city's regaining the franchise that had gone by the boards three years earlier in 1950.

A Hero on the Battlefield, Too
After graduating from Antioch (California) High School, Gino Marchetti fought in the Battle of the Bulge during World War II. He was only 18 years old.

Q17 The first points scored by the Colts in Super Bowl V were the result of a Johnny Unitas pass that caromed off two players and came to rest in John Mackey's hands. Name the duo who touched the ball before it got to the tight end.

Q18 Johnny Unitas was knocked out of Super Bowl V in the second quarter due to a hard tackle. Who bruised his ribs with the hit?

Q19 The Colts were down 13–6 with eight minutes left in the fourth quarter of Super Bowl V when Craig Morton threw an interception. Who snared the Cowboy pass to turn Baltimore's fortunes around?

Q20 With the score knotted at 13 late in the fourth quarter of Super Bowl V, the game seem destined for overtime. Whose interception with 1:09 left led to the game-winning field goal?

Q21 What was the distance on the Super Bowl V-winning field goal that Jim O'Brien lofted through the Orange Bowl uprights?

Q22 How many turnovers were committed by the Colts and Cowboys in Super Bowl V?

Q23 Considered one of the most competitive Super Bowls in NFL annals, the Colts edged Dallas to take Super Bowl V, 16–13. How much was the first-place prize in that historic contest?

Q24 The setting was Memorial Stadium for the AFC playoff encounter between the Colts and Raiders in 1977. An Errol Mann field goal with 26 seconds in regulation knotted the game, and in OT, the Raiders won, 37–31. How many quarters did it take to complete one of the longest games ever played?

TRADES, WAIVES, AND ACQUISITIONS

Q1 The Colts tapped the Heisman Trophy winner in the first round of the 1953 draft, but the Oklahoma product turned his back on the team and signed with the Edmonton Eskimos. Who distinguished himself in the Great White North?

Q2 In the famous five-for-10 trade of 1953, two eventual NFL head coaches were principals in the transaction. Who were the 15 men involved in the swap with Cleveland?

BALTIMORE COLTS

A17   Colt Eddie Hinton
Cowboy cornerback Mel Renfro

A18   George Andrie

A19   Rick Volk (after the pass bounced off the fingertips of Walt Garrison)

A20   Mike Curtis's

A21   32 yards

A22   11

A23 $15,000

A24   Six (Ken Stabler hit Dave Casper for a 10-yard score in the sixth quarter.)

A1   Billy Vessels

A2   Baltimore received Don Shula, Harry Agganis, Bert Reichlar, Carl Taseff, Gern Nagler, Elmer Willhoite, Ed Sharkey, Art Spinney, Dick Batten, and Stu Sheetz in return for Mike McCormack, Tom Catlin, Hershel Forrester, John Petibon, and Don Colo.

TRADES, WAIVES, AND ACQUISITIONS

Q3   From what team was Jimmy Orr obtained in 1960 as part of the Dig Daddy Lipscomb trade?

Q4   In the winter of 1961, the Colts traded Jackie Simpson for Billy Ray Smith. With what team did the Hosses do business?

Q5   What dual-purpose player did the Colts obtain in a deal with Pittsburgh for Marv Woodson and Bill Saul before the 1964 season?

Q6   Who came to the Colts in 1970 after the team sent Ocie Austin and Preston Pearson to Pittsburgh in a deal with the Steelers?

Q7   Which Colt QB came to the team in exchange for John Andrews in a 1972 deal with the Chargers?

Q8   Whom did the Colts ship to the Left Coast in order to acquire Raymond Chester in a 1973 deal with the Oakland Raiders?

Q9   Jim Cheyunski, Mike Montler, and Halvor Hagen were acquired from the Bills for linebackers Edgar Chandler and Jeff Lyman. What other player shuffled off to Buffalo in the 1975 trade?

Q10   Picked in the top round of the 1976 draft by San Diego, this back came to the Colts in a trade two years later for Lydell Mitchell. Who was he?

Q11   What did the Colts receive from Denver in exchange for John Elway in the may 1983 blockbuster deal with the Broncos?

Q12   The Colts obtained Raul Allegre in 1983 in return for a draft choice. With what team did Baltimore do business?

BALTIMORE COLTS

A3   Pittsburgh Steelers

A4   Pittsburgh Steelers

A5   Lou Michaels (kicker and defensive end)

A6   Ray May

A7   Marty Domres

A8   Bubba Smith

A9   Wayne Patrick

A10   Joe Washington

A11   Chris Hinton
Mark Herrmann
Number one draft pick in 1984

A12   Dallas Cowboys

Sports Books Ordering Information

Ask for any of the books listed below at your bookstore. Or to order direct from the publisher, call 1-800-447-BOOK (MasterCard or Visa), or send a check or money order for the books purchased (plus $3.00 shipping and handling for the first book ordered and 50¢ for each additional book) to Carol Publishing Group, 120 Enterprise Avenue, Dept. 1424, Secaucus, NJ 07094.

Settle-Your-Bet Sports Trivia Books

Questions, Answers (and Photos) Covering Every Professional Sport Team--Past & Present--From the Following Cities:

Boston Sports Quiz by Brenda Alesii & Daniel Locche; Paperback $9.95 (#51212)

Chicago Sports Quiz by Brenda Alesii & Daniel Locche; Paperback $9.95 (#51372)

Los Angeles Sports Quiz by Brenda Alesii & Daniel Locche; Paperback $10.95 (#51381)

New York Sports Quiz by Brenda Alesii & Daniel Locche; Paperback $10.95 (#51215)

Philadelphia Sports Quiz by Brenda Alesii & Daniel Locche; Paperback $9.95 (#51416)

The Ultimate Sports Trivia Book: The Official Bar Book of Runyon's Saloon by Jim Benagh & Tim Hays; Paperback $8.95 (#51273)

Washington/Baltimore Sports Quiz by Brenda Alesii & Daniel Locche; Paperback $9.95 (#51424)

Tennis Books

Love Match: Nelson vs. Navratilova by Sandra Faulkner w/Judy Nelson; Hardcover w/16 pages of photos. $19.95 (#72157)

Winning Ugly: Mental Warfare in Tennis by Brad Gilbert & Steve Jamison; Hardcover w/8 pages of photos. $18.95 (#72169)

World Tennis Magazine's Guide to the Best Tennis Resorts by Peter Coan w/Barry Stambler; Paperback $10.95 (#51272)

Sports Jokes

The World's Greatest Golf Jokes Compiled and edited by Stan McDougal; Paperback, with illustrations throughout. $4.50 (#62502)

(Prices subject to change; books subject to availability)

Boxing Books

The Autobiography of Jack Johnson: In the Ring and Out; Paperback, illustrated w/ photos throughout. $10.95 (#51358)

Boxing Babylon: Behind the Shadowy World of the Prize Ring by Nigel Collins; Hardcover, illustrated w/photos throughout. $18.95 (#51183)

Mike Tyson: Money, Myth & Betrayal by Monteith Illingworth; Hardcover w/8 pages of photos. $22.95 (#72079)

Muhammad Ali: A View From the Corner by Ferdie Pacheco; Hardcover, illustrated w/ photos throughout. $21.95 (#72100)

A Pictorial History of Boxing: Revised and Updated Edition by Sam Andre & Nat Fleischer, updated by Peter Arnold; *Illustrated w/ nearly 2000 photos & prints.* Oversized paperback. $19.95 (#51427)

Baseball Books

Dodgers: The First 100 Years by Stanley Cohen; Paperback, illustrated w/photos throughout. $4.50 (#62508)

Five O'Clock Lightning: Ruth, Gehrig, DiMaggio and the Glory Years of the New York Yankees by Tommy Henrich w/Bill Gilbert; Hardcover w/8 pages of photos. $19.95 (#72101)

Great Moments in Baseball: From the World Series of 1903 to the Modern Records of Nolan Ryan by Tom Seaver w/ Marty Appel; Hardcover w/photos throughout. $19.95 (#72095)

Say It Ain't So, Joe: The True Story of Shoeless Joe Jackson, revised edition by Donald Gropman; Paperback w/16 pages of photos. $10.95 (#51336)